EXTRAORDINARY WOMEN

INSPIRATIONAL WOMEN REVEAL THEIR JOURNEYS TO SUCCESS

POWERHOUSE PUBLICATIONS

www.powerhousepublishing.com

COPYRIGHT

Powerhouse Publications
Suite 124. 94 London Road
Headington, Oxford
OX3 9FN

www.powerhousepublishing.com

CONTENTS

INTRODUCTION

A good book is the ultimate mentor. When you read a powerful book, it can open up doors you didn't even know existed. It can change your way of thinking and spark you into action. It can help you find the shortcuts in less time. It can transform your career, your relationships, your finances. In short, it can alter the course of your life.

I know this from personal experience as I once resigned from a prestigious job at Oxford University after reading a book. Everyone thought I was stark raving mad at the time – I was told in no uncertain terms that no one at my level usually resigned. It seemed that you were expected to either retire or die in the job. I could so easily have stayed there, oblivious, in my golden handcuffs. But that book opened up new possibilities for me. It showed me how to think bigger than I'd ever thought before. It showed me an alternative way of living. It gave me permission to do the unthinkable.

Imagine what would have happened if I hadn't read that book! I suspect that I might still be in that job today – working frequent unpaid overtime; receiving two-hour phone calls at home on Sundays; spending evenings and weekends away from my three children; dealing with politics, back-stabbing, and student dramas.

I wouldn't even have been aware of the exciting future that was waiting for me.

As the author Helen Exley once said: "Books can be dangerous. The best ones should be labelled: This could change your life." *Extraordinary Women* is one such book. It has already brought about two momentous changes in my life before it's even published. I won't share what these changes are with you as it might be a spoiler for the book. And the life lessons that we each take away are likely to be different. So I'll leave you to make your own discoveries.

If you're feeling stuck, I urge you to read this book. If you're wanting to step up to the next level, read this book. If you're feeling ahead of your game, read this book. There is something in it for everyone.

Write notes. Extract the wisdom. Implement what you're learning. Absorb the lessons in your bloodstream. Take action. Then, see for yourself how much your life changes.

Enjoy!

Stephanie J. Hale

Powerhouse Publications

NICOLA WHITING

"We are relied upon and trusted by the most secure organisations in the world – people like the Department of Defence, the FBI, and a whole host of globally-recognised clients."

Job Title: Chief Strategy Officer, Titania Ltd

Personal Bio: Experienced Chief Operations and Strategy Officer with a strong history of working in Cyber Security / InfoSec. Specialisms include enterprise security automation software (self-healing networks), business development, trust-based selling, and neuromarketing.

An advocate for autism and women in cyber, she provides government-level advice on diversity and is Worcestershire's Commissioner for the UK Cyber Science and Innovation Audit.

She is an engaging public speaker and writes for publications such as *The Huffington Post, Defence Contracts Bulletin, Defence News Online, and Signal.* Keynote topics include "The Rise of Automated Attacks", "The Future of Automated Cyber Defences", and "Hacking the Human Brain".

In 2017, Nicola was named by SC Magazine as one of the Top 20 most influential women working in cyber security.

Business: Titania Group — Award-winning security software solutions

Products: Accurate configuration and compliance auditing software that can automatically find and fix network security gaps – before hackers can exploit them. Titania's automation tools are depended upon to achieve secure networks by global organisations in over 90 countries.

Clients include: Department of Defence, UK Government, FBI, PayPal, Cisco, BT, Deloitte, and KPMG.

Awards: Winner of 48 industry awards including The Queen's Award for Enterprise in Innovation.

Contact: T: +44 (0)1905 888785

E: enquiries@titania.com

Website: www.titania.com

♦ ♦ ♦

Everyone has a story. Some stories start with silver spoons and finish with Ugg boots and double caramel macchiatos. Mine didn't. If yours didn't either, I've found that that's okay. It's okay because you get to create your own journey, your own story, and your own 'happy ending'.

My story begins with Mum. She was new to the army base, and training for a nursing career, when she was charmed by an officer. At 18, she was suddenly pregnant, jobless, and the fresh recipient of 'honourable discharge' papers. He got posted to Germany with his pregnant wife and children who (as they lived off base) he'd conveniently neglected to mention. Mum travelled to Shropshire, to a special place tucked away in Much Wenlock – a place you put babies up for adoption. That's where I was born.

Mum doesn't talk about it much. When she does, she focuses on the camaraderie of the ward, of all the girls in the same position. What I imagine knowing Mum now, though, is how hard it must have been. I imagine her wondering if the other girls felt like she did, and if their eyes were dark-ringed. I wonder if the nurses reminded her of her discharge papers, sitting at home, and thinking of what could have been.

When she describes my birth, she talks about the dramatics of the large Italian woman in labour opposite her. I see her, dark hair plastered to her face, hands gripping as she frantically puffs before the pain then, when it comes, screaming at the top of her lungs and swearing loudly in Italian. My mum laughs and I laugh with her, but she never describes her own pain or what she went through and I try not to ask. I can tell it upsets her – even now. I know she must have been brave; I know she is strong.

In 1970 it wasn't easy: there was social stigma around being an unwed mother. But after my birth, she didn't want to give me up. When Mum told my grandparents over the phone, they said, "Thank God!" They'd both wanted to keep me but hadn't wanted to pressure her and were so relieved. Being kept was my first major blessing. We travelled back from Shropshire as a family, back to Mum's home town, Worcester, and a local council estate.

There were estates like it all over the country – the 'before' pictures of urban regeneration. Dines Green had high unemployment, transit vans on lawns, drugs, drunks, and domestic violence. I saw it all growing up: it was the background noise for a rough estate during the 1970s and 1980s. It wasn't something that bothered me. It also had its very own dedicated police station – the police didn't have to travel far when nicking someone! At one stage, there were six of us in a three-bedroom council house – three generations – my grandparents, my mum, my aunt, my cousin, and me.

I can't remember how we fitted in. Trying to find space in a house that full was hard.

My first mentor was my grandfather, Frank. I was under five and he created the foundation of who I am. He'd been a soldier, a bugler in the army, and he'd served overseas in some pretty horrendous wars. He was a Salvationist and had been in the Salvation Army. He was an artist and musician; he was creative and caring, and just amazing. He encouraged everyone, including Mum, to be the best they could be. She did her nursing training outside the army – she achieved what she wanted to, even with a young child. She passed that on to me. I've always been very driven to better myself, which I guess came from my grandfather.

When he came out of the army, he drove lorries to support his family and travelled up and down the country. Mum told me that sometimes she'd even been taken with him. She said lorry drivers *always* know where the best cheap food stops are and described sitting in his cab, eating bacon butties with her dad. Even now, wherever I'm travelling, whatever the country, if I see a load of trucks parked up next to a local eatery, I think, "good food, served cheap". If I'm hungry, that's where I pull over – it's a top tip.

When I was little, 'Grandad Frank' was the driver on our camping trips to the seaside. There weren't a lot of those; they were special. We'd leave matching footprints on the shore as we scooped up perfect sea-washed sand for our castles, leaving the waves to fill the holes we left behind. In those pictures, he's in shirt sleeves and rolled-up trousers; in almost all the others he's wearing his button-up cardigan (whose buttons reminded me of footballs). In all of them, his ever-present cigarette is dangling from his mouth. I remember those buttons, but I don't remember the cigarettes – that's basically what took him from us. He got lung cancer.

I know that even during some of the most challenging times of his life, my grandfather was still giving, still positive, and still generous. I was only young, but I can't ever remember him talking about pain.

When he got cancer, he had the room above the stairs with the big bunker in it. That was where his little single bed was and everyone else just fitted around that. I'd go and sit on his bed because I wanted quiet and he'd tell me stories. He'd draw for me and use tiny Airfix paint pots, with fine little brushes to paint cowboys, horses, and amazing things on the wall. He used to get me to tell stories too – and he listened. He taught me to read and encouraged me to learn, and asked questions. He was a real inspiration. He formed my personality. When he died, I cried for more days than I've cried for anybody else in my entire life. I was five – losing him was huge.

When he died, Mum's nursing training came in handy. She became the main breadwinner and family income provider. She was a single parent, but you got more money if you worked night shifts, so that's what she did. I snatched time with her in the mornings, the evenings, and on weekends, but she was often tired, just getting up or returning from work. My mum was a nurse right up until I went to school; she's a natural carer and she loved nursing. She left when she felt the staffing levels meant she couldn't look after people properly any more.

Music was another one of her joys. When my mum would sing, everyone stopped to listen. She could have sung professionally, but it didn't guarantee consistent income and as a single parent she needed it. I'd go with her to the folk clubs and sit in the back, talking in between sets. She sang at Glastonbury and when I was older she travelled around Europe with a band. Mum is a real inspiration; she sacrificed so much to raise and support me.

I suppose in terms of childhood my biggest influence came from my grandfather having travelled in the army and being a Salvationist. He had a more philosophical, wider world view than would be typical in the estate where we lived – that's what he taught me. I could open a book and be anywhere I wanted to go, learn from anyone I wanted to learn from – it was a great gift. In contrast, my grandmother was really home-focused, a real matriarch, so if my cousin and I misbehaved, she'd be the one chasing us down the garden with the washing stick or whatever she could get her hands on. Thankfully, we were fast runners so she didn't often catch us. She was more hot-tempered, more explosive as a person, but really hard working. She used to work in the local greengrocers. She'd carry sacks of spuds. We lost her to cancer too, but a lot later. I was in my twenties when she passed on. So that was my childhood.

My life lessons began before I left school. My family taught me that money was something you earned. That was really visible throughout my childhood because they were all grafters, whether it was my gran hauling potato sacks, or my grandfather driving lorries, or my mum working nights to make sure we still had days at the seaside. Whatever it was, that was the ethic. If you wanted pocket money, you earned it, even if it was in silly little ways. I can remember being so excited when the Corona pop bottle man came around because my cousin Jo and I were each allowed to return the bottles and collect our prized ten-penny pieces. We'd take them straight round to the local shop and trade them for sweets.

School, I tended to block out. When you are somebody who wants to learn, wants to grow, and you're in a council estate school, it's not a pleasant experience. Bullying was common. Standing outside the crowd is not an easy thing to do when you have that kind of background. You have to be pretty determined to continually put yourself up to that. I learned how to hide quite quickly so I'd often be found in the cloakroom hiding in between two coats, reading a book, hoping I wouldn't stand out. So, that wasn't awesome.

Music changed all that. Secondary school brought music lessons and I discovered I adored singing properly, publicly, with groups of other people. It was encouraged by a wonderful teacher, who I adored. Music brought me into a different realm; through it, I found people at school who shared my passions.

Report cards changed from 'Nicola doesn't mix well' to 'Nicola is a lively soul' – music made me shine. I got involved in the local church choir, in fact more than one. I'd catch lifts with the choir master to other church services just so I could sing. Well, you can't do all that praising without wondering a little about God and there I was, a teenage girl, without a father.

I started reading and analysing The Bible. I took 2 Corinthians 6:18 as a pretty literal invite. It says, *"And I will be a Father to you, and you will be my sons and daughters, says the Lord Almighty."* So, if He picked me, I figured it would be okay if I picked Him right back. Some of you may think that's a little odd, but to me it made sense. My real dad had let us down badly. I needed a father I could trust, somebody that I could turn to, someone who I could be honest with – here was a Father with a capital F who really fitted that bill. He'd left invites scattered through His book. He wanted children. It made sense; it seemed a no brainer.

God had always been in my life up until that point (through the influence of my grandfather), but I had never really engaged with Him personally until my teens. It made me a different person. I thought if Jesus was my big brother, I'd better start learning the 'family values'. My grandfather laid the foundations, but becoming a Christian made them concrete. Lots of study later and I'd honed it into three rules: *1. Do good, 2. Forgive everyone (including yourself),* and 3. *Treat others as you'd like to be treated.* I'm still guided by those values I set all those years ago. I don't always get it right; I often fail. But I try – and that's all anyone can do.

By 16, I was working evenings and weekends quite regularly. One of my first jobs, in the kitchens at an old people's home, was where I saw my first dead body. It was macaroni cheese night, a resident favourite: it was bland, comforting, and kind to false teeth. I stood there with my heavy tray wondering if I should wake her before it went cold before realising that she wasn't sleeping. I took the tray back to chef and said she wouldn't need her mac'n'cheese and they gave me a half-day off in case I was traumatised. In reality, I wasn't. Things like that didn't affect me.

On a council estate, in the 1970s and 1980s, there were 'domestics' that people didn't want to report. They sometimes made their way to Mum's nursing hands so it was just a fact of life. There were too many pubs in the area, too many drugs, and too many people out of work – but even though those things were true, people still helped each other out. You did what you could and families and neighbours stuck together.

At 17, I was studying for my 'A' levels and working late nights in a fish and chip shop. It often meant serving drunks who came out of the pubs and it gave me my own 'Crocodile Dundee' moment. One of them decided he wanted money, probably for drugs (he looked more than drunk). I worked with an 18-year-old lad called Linden who was serving in the front while I was cutting up chickens in the back. I was portioning them with this big 12-inch blade: it had to be pretty big to break through the breast bones of chickens. I heard, "Nic! Nic! Nic!" He sounded panicked so I strode to the front of the shop where the counter was, and there was this guy brandishing a penknife. Linden said, "He wants the money from the till." I was standing there in an apron covered in chicken gizzards with a massive 12-inch knife. I looked at his knife and then my knife, walked up to the till, and turned the key so it locked. Then, I threw the key into the chip fryer and said to the guy, "Help yourself, I'm off to phone the police." He just ran out, and Linden stood there looking at me like a goldfish out of water. I said, "Well, you might as well drain the fryer. I'm off to cut the chickens up." I left him fishing the key out with a bent bit of wire so it could cool down and we could carry on serving.

I've done all kinds of things since those early 'no experience required' jobs. I've worked selling cars and selling corrugated cardboard boxes, I've sold advertising and worked in distribution. There's stuff I've loved about every role. I learned what makes a good cardboard box, how packaging impacts how people's food is delivered, and how manufacturers save money by making tiny design changes. It can make them millions. All that stuff was absorbed early on as part of quite low-level jobs. If your mind is open and you ask the right questions, you can learn things from whatever you do and whoever you interact with. It's amazing how much you learn. If you don't believe this, then think about what working in McDonalds could teach you about process automation or go and watch 'The Founder' movie – it's enlightening.

The BIG defining moment in my life was something completely unexpected and very, very transformative. I was in my teens in church, going through the motions as people do, just trying to be a better person, and we all knelt down to pray. My mind was wandering a bit. I wasn't really fully focused on anything, but I was suddenly filled with love from an external source. There's no way of explaining it. Imagine one of those plastic funnels that you use to fill containers – it was like I couldn't hold enough love and I was just being filled up. I loved everybody in that church, even the people I really didn't get on with or didn't like. It was such an amazing feeling and it only lasted for probably seconds, but it felt like forever. There isn't a way that I could explain it. There's no way that doing nothing and then suddenly feeling like that can be explained. I wasn't ill. I wasn't sick or running a fever. I wasn't in the throes of some kind of ecstatic, everybody jumping up and down and waving arms type of religious service. I was just kneeling, about to pray, and it just happened and then it went away.

I just sat there and the prayers were happening around me. I felt like, "Well, what was that? Where did that come from?" The only conclusion was that was what God was like. And I thought, "If that's the kind of love that's out there, WOW!" So that's when I joined loads of choirs, because I wanted to sing. I wanted to praise. I wanted to go, "Wow, that's amazing." I was also insufferable, just like when you fall in love with anybody. You'd want to talk to everybody about the new love of your life. You don't want to spend time talking about anything else and you just become annoying. (I learnt later that if you want someone to listen to you, then you must first learn to listen to them. Listening is a great way to express love!)

To know with absolute conviction that there's something bigger than you is a defining moment. It's just the most amazing gift a human being can get. I didn't know what I was supposed to do with this gift. I didn't know if I was supposed to become a vicar. I thought, "What does this mean? Not a lot of people get given this. Does that mean I'm somehow chosen? Does that mean I'm special?" I was only 17, so it wasn't like I was a deep philosopher. I just knew that I was suddenly in love with something that was bigger than me. What I started to do was spend time in religious areas to try and just have space because, if you remember, my home was full of people. A house full of people doesn't really lend itself to quiet, contemplative thought. I'd find myself going to churches and tucking myself into the back to just give myself some thinking space. Not because it was a religious space, but because they're normally pretty empty and quiet. I'd go to libraries and sit down there, but that wasn't the same. It was still too busy. While I was doing these things, I met the precentor of Worcester Cathedral, James Butterworth. He had heard me sing because I used to go to the cathedral to sing and he offered to give me free singing lessons. They were proper singing lessons and it was in this amazing house that was off Worcester Cathedral with a big piano. I was like, "This is amazing. Look at this life."

I started spending time with people who lived and worked around the cathedral. These were middle-class, well-educated people, with degrees. I'd get invited to dinner. I'd make friends with their teenage daughters. They were all good, Christian, caring people. They invited me into their homes, lent me books, they wanted to help me grow into the person I was saying I wanted to be. Their surroundings were strange to me. I'd find things out like, "Oh, they're all sitting down and there's more than one knife and fork here. We're not eating on the sofa, it's on the table. How do I do this?" The average 17-year-old isn't reading books on etiquette that they've got out of the library, working out how to fit in socially with a different way of doing things. I was.

That was, again, another thing that was pretty transformative. The people I knew on the council estate had horizons like, "I want to be the manager of the shop I work in." Versus, "I'd like to be the Bishop of Worcester" or "help kids in Africa" or be whatever else you wanted to be. I saw them learning for the joy of learning, then having conversations about politics, history, and things that were serious 'big world' events. I hadn't had that before, but I liked it a lot. It made me feel like I wanted to stretch myself. It made me feel like anything could be achieved if you just believed that you could do it. That, combined with my belief that somebody had my back, was really life-changing.

There's a book called *The Go-Giver,* by a guy called Bob Burg. I found it not many years ago. It's the principle of how I got to where I am today, which is by focusing on what can I give. How can I be the best at whatever job I'm in? How can I deliver more? How can I be better? The focus is always on other people.

By my 30s, I was the chairman of a jewellery guild, a writer, a teacher, and a business owner. Then my previous husband told me that he loved me, but not as a wife any more. We separated and I sold my business. I basically left all that behind because it was part of that life. I was like, “Okay. I’m going to make a new life, I'll go back to Worcester.” So, I did.

I bought the scraggiest flat you can imagine, but it was one that I could buy outright. It had horrible floors. It needed re-wiring. It needed a new kitchen. It had urine-soaked floors where they’d kept pets indoors. It was just the most disgusting thing you have ever seen in your life, but it was mine – I was back on the property ladder and I had plans...

In the middle of renovating the flat, I connected with an old friend of mine, who asked if I could meet up for lunch. It was a last-minute thing. I was renovating a property without an income and had a limited budget so I suggested Pizza Hut across the road: “Yeah. Okay. We'll go across and I'll have a salad bar and a bit of pizza.”

While we were there, she was busy talking about some of the problems she was facing. She was in a company that had an amazing product, but they didn't really know how to sell it. She didn't really have any salespeople and although her husband (the guy that ran it) was a technical genius, he felt that when people phoned up to buy their software, they were just interrupting his coding time.

Using my experience of all the jobs that I had done, what I did was to start mapping out – literally on the back of the famous napkin – how the company was probably going to grow. “You're going to need some salespeople, and that first salesperson probably needs to be the sort of person that could expand into managing a team. They would grow that part of the business for you because you haven't got in-house expertise. You're probably going to need some finance people; you're probably going to need a marketing team at some stage." I was effectively mapping out all the divisions of their future company.

By doing a bit of 'go-giving', rather than focusing on my impending divorce and splitting up, I'd helped my friend. She'd basically said, "These are the problems I'm having. Can you help me?" and I'd said, "Okay." She insisted that the guy who coded all this software, Ian, drop his dinner and come to Pizza Hut. I wasn't really that keen on it because I was sitting there in an old tracksuit covered in plaster dust and bits of paint. I'd only popped out to have lunch with a friend in a gap between working and carrying sacks of plaster up the stairs. Suddenly, I was in a business meeting. She was quite insistent. That's the first time I met Ian, who was quite grumpy because he hadn't eaten yet and we were already hitting desserts.

I talked about it again, and said, "Look, I'm just giving you some ideas on the back of a napkin. If you want I'll come in, meet up with you guys when I'm better dressed, more focused, and I can talk through this properly and maybe give you some ideas as to what this salesperson might look like. Sales, growing sales, that's the area I feel most confident in and maybe I can give you some tips about what that job description might look like. If you really want, I'll come in and help you interview them." They loved the idea, so over the weekend I put some ideas together.

I went in fully prepared to tell them about the person they needed to have, but they basically just wanted me to work for them and be that person. I said, "I don't have a bedroom to sleep in, I haven't got a floor in my living room, and I don't own a bath at the moment. I'm running to my mum's for showers. It's not a good time for me." They said, "No. We want you." Because they were a start-up, they offered me a ridiculously low salary which I couldn't have lived on. So, I said, "Not me. Too busy. At least two months before I could even contemplate it." They said, "That's okay. We'll wait." I said, "It's not enough money. I could get more money working in the Co-op. I don't need a lot, but I do need this much because that's my minimum to eat, work, sleep, run a house. There you go." So, they said yes and they gave me my minimum amount of money, with commission.

I joined Titania as the third employee: the first people had been Alen – another developer like Ian (who now heads our development team) – and Ruth, a really talented young English graduate who I became firm friends with. Ruth is a true 'go-giver', she puts her heart and soul into everything she does, I admire her immensely, and today she's our Operational MD.

The company started growing quite rapidly, to a point where I was being overly successful. We couldn't grow the business because the 'growth money' was coming to me in commission. So, I went to them with a proposal to cut my commission and increase my base salary and to use the income they were taking off me to fund another person that could help grow sales. They were shocked. "What? You want to cut your own income to add a person to our company?" I said, "Yes, that's what I want to do."

It illustrates what happens with 'go-giving' because I was thinking, "What does the company need? They need to do this, in order to achieve that." So, Ian was the main person I needed to persuade because he couldn't see why we needed another sales person at the time. I wasn't sophisticated or subtle: I said, "Look, I'm paying for it. You're only really saying 'yes' to six months of this person, because that's their six-month probation period. If it doesn't work out, then they won't have justified their own income and you'll still be better off because you'll be paying me less overall." It was a bit of a no-brainer, but I set it up as I really wanted it to happen. It did, and that was the first salesperson other than me. Then, the company grew exactly as predicted in terms of departments. My job in Titania has been about building teams and putting processes together while allowing Ian to be a creative genius and to run the technical side without having to worry about salespeople.

That's what I've done: to build the people side of the company, to help make that 'back of a napkin' growth plan a reality. My main role was to find amazing people and let them replace me; I've basically replaced myself in almost every key area. Ruth, that second employee who was there when I joined, has been a true partner in that. We have a productive and supportive leadership team who work really well together. Ian our founder and CEO, Ruth our Operational MD, Shelley our HR manager, Vaughan our CTO, and Phil our CFO who's replacing me as COO. There's only one person missing – an experienced CMO, but I'm sure they'll come along and I know they'll be just the right person!

My next role, having formed a lot of the teams to the point where we don't need to be involved, is 'crystal ball predictor'. I'm looking forward to coming full circle, to being less operational and more strategic. I started off as Chief Sales Officer, CSO, and I'll end up as Chief Strategy Officer, CSO. It's perfect.

Along the way, my friend and Ian broke up. It wasn't the first time, but she needed a new start. I'm very grateful that she suggested Ian ask me out on a date: by then we were very much business partners. Now we're partners in every sense of the word and I co-own the company. My little 'go-give' in Pizza Hut has given me a new life, a new soulmate, and a new home. I owe Titania and its people such a lot: they're fantastic, they're colleagues and friends, and they feel like family.

Titania only has four 'family values'. I'm proud to say they were chosen by the team and are the core of who we are and how we operate. The first one is to '*Choose Positivity*'. We understand that if you're somebody that suffers from depression, being positive can be impossible. But choosing positivity means just choosing to be the most positive person you can be that day and bring that with you.

The second one is to '*Be a Titan*' – deriving from Titania – and I love it. The word Titan makes you think of something strong and towering and defendable. For us, it means bringing your best self, being accountable, and using the collective genius of the other people in the team. Being a Titan is being your own cheerleader and being other people's cheerleader too!

The third value is '*Go-Give*', and that's about how we treat each other. In many ways, it's about going, 'Okay. What can I do for this person? What can I do for my clients? What is it that I can do to serve them best?' Actually, if you are surrounded by people who are doing that, you benefit too. You'll propagate an environment of mutual respect and support, drive team culture, and ultimately drive growth. 'Go-giving' is the spirit of Titania: doing our best to serve our team and our clients has resulted in all our greatest successes.

The last value is to '*Have Fun*'. That's about celebrating our success and saying, "Okay, we work really hard. Let's play hard." Our team chooses to go camping with each other. They choose to meet up after work. They choose to go and support each other's poetry slams. They choose to celebrate birthdays. They choose to celebrate success. At Titania, we read out all the positive feedback and thanks that clients continually send us in our company meetings. We're constantly focused on who we want to be, who we are, and how we celebrate that. I think that really helps drive us forward as a business.

Titania's 'family business' is in creating software that automates network security and defence. We make life simpler for people by managing and protecting the world's most complex networks and releasing them from a massive amount of their workload. We are relied upon and trusted by the most secure organisations in the world – people like the

Department of Defence, the FBI, and a whole host of globally-recognised clients. But why?

I could talk about our technology. It's pretty impressive and unique, fixing a problem with getting granular accuracy into automated security tools that has plagued our industry for decades. However, for many people 'cyber' is something that you see on Hollywood TV shows or wonder about if your bank gets hacked or your data gets stolen. So, I'm not going to get technical and talk about configuration auditing, artificial intelligence, or chasms in data accuracy – instead I'll use an analogy that makes sense for everyone.

Almost every individual or business takes the risk of fire far more seriously than the risk of a cyber-attack. No one would leave petrol-soaked rags by their front door, let alone add a convenient lighter or a pile of matches, but we do it every day with the systems that are essential to our lives and businesses. We leave undefended risks everywhere...

Using our fire analogy, the bad guys would be like, "Okay, I can burn this building down with matches. I can burn it down with cigarette lighters. I can burn it down with this incendiary device. I can burn it down using petrol." But essentially, the defenders just have to realise that all of that will be solved by not leaving flammable stuff lying around and adding a really good fire detection and prevention system. The challenge is that most people haven't really understood that yet. They're still wondering, "How do I defend against a lighter? How do I defend against an incendiary device? How do I defend against petrol?" Well, it's actually a couple of core things that pretty much defend against most of that stuff.

That's essentially what Titania helps people with. Our software finds the flammable stuff on your networks (all those little gaps in security that nothing else spots) and helps you get rid of it. We automate the essential 'health and safety' actions you need to maintain network security. It's really valuable and exciting work.

Aside from my work with Titania, I've had a few other key successes and achievements over the years. They've all been around the same area: my key skills are in finding new ways of working with people or putting people together. When I was in car sales, I worked for Smart: I was outselling some of London dealerships from this one in Nottingham and they couldn't work out why. The spikes in our figures were so odd that we ended up with Smart Germany starting to ask, "Why's that happening?" and our dealership network were asking the same question.

People travelled from all over the country to come and buy Smart cars from me in Nottingham. It was because I'd identified a gap in the marketplace. I knew there were a whole host of people who had Smart cars who didn't want to just buy a yellow one, a silver one, or a black one. They wanted a red one with black spots on it that looked like a ladybug or they wanted one that looked like a tiger. These were quirky little cars that appealed to people with quirky personalities: artists, musicians, and people that had a need to be creative. People who wanted a more customised look, but for it to still be economical.

There was a Smart car forum called the Smart Owners' Club. It was all very official, but they had people that kept saying, "I'd like to remap it, change the paint, and put a big sound system in." The company's answer was, "You shouldn't do that, it will invalidate your warranty." I looked at these people and thought, "Yeah, I'm one of you guys. I'm one of the outskirts people that wants a pink car that rides like a rocket." I created a forum called Smart Maniacs and made it free and said, "Right, okay, you weirdos like me, come and join." It was about being a community of like-minded people. It wasn't about me, it was about them, and they owned it. I became part of the moderation team, to ensure that people acted with decency and integrity towards each other. If people really got antsy, I'd say, "Look. I'm going to let you cool down by blocking you for a little while, and when you've decided what you want to do, come back."

To make their dreams come true, I built a relationship with a local Smart car specialist garage in Nottingham. It was not part of the dealership, but it did painting, leatherwork, custom exhausts, and remapping – all of which were not approved by Smart. I was really honest with the customers. I would say to them, "Look, if you want a red one with black polka dots, I can sell you a red one and connect you to a great graphics person who'll create you a ladybird. If you want a pink one, I can introduce you to a place that can paint your panels pink, it'll cost you this much. They're a garage I trust, and I'm happy to introduce you to them. I'm happy to facilitate the conversation if you want me to." They'd go, "That's amazing. That's what I want." If they talked about remapping or delimiting the engine, I'd say, "There's a risk of you blowing your engine up and you will invalidate the warranty. This is how much a new engine will cost and here's the potential risk." I'd just be really honest and transparent.

These are the foundations that Titania is built on: we all believe in selling through trust and building trusting relationships. I did that naturally. That was before I found *The Go-Giver*, before I learned about trusted relationship selling. It was just who I was, but what that meant was I could outsell London because people who wanted different cars would find Smart Maniacs. Without realising what I was doing, I was building a following of raving fans. I was focused on them achieving their vision, finding ways to work within the parameters I had to deliver for them. They brought me referral after referral.

When Smart came to visit me, to ask where all the sales were coming from, they asked, "Why is this happening?" So, I walked them through it, and they said, "But that invalidates the warranty," and I said, "Yep. I tell them that. I've got it in emails, me telling them." They were asking, "But why do they want a pink one?" And I answered, "Because that's what they want."

My biggest achievement was when Smart introduced custom colours globally. It was only on their Smart Brabus cars (their most expensive model), but it was in almost any colour you wanted. It was really exciting. I instigated a global change in Smart just by being a go-giver and a little, trust-based seller in Nottingham. That wasn't my intention, but that's what happened. Little things, done consistently, can make big changes because people look at the results. I've had a number of situations like that.

The things I'm proudest of, my biggest successes, are when I've built communities or inspired people in some way. Even with Titania, we're still in touch with people who have spun off and become entrepreneurs. They've been really kind to us and have come back and said, "You made a difference. You made an impact. You changed my view of certain things and made me a little bit more of the person that I am." I don't think there's a bigger gift. It's what my grandfather Frank did for me and that made me who I am. The thought that I'm doing that for other people, even in small ways, is pretty humbling, pretty moving. So, I think my biggest success and achievements have always been about other people.

My biggest message for anyone who would like to achieve success is to use *compound interest* in your own humanity and growth. Warren Buffet did it in finance: he took his initial investment and kept growing it, over and over again, in a continual but gradual process. He's now one of the richest men on the planet – his net worth is over $80 billion. So, imagine what compound interest could do, if you continually invested in yourself.

Mentors are a great way to accelerate self-investment success. Whatever your chosen path, imagine all the insights and advice you could get from someone who's ahead of you and on the same journey. If you can't find a mentor or are worried about approaching the wrong person, then some of the greatest mentors in the world are available *for free* from your local library. Yes, many of the richest, most successful people in the world have written their ‘stories’ down, including all their best life lessons and mistakes. (N.B. If, like me, you turn down corners, make notes, and read with highlighter pens, it’s probably best to get your own books from Amazon.)

My top mentoring book was *How to Win Friends and Influence People* by Dale Carnegie, a man who Warren Buffet said changed his life. The book talks about getting out of mental ruts and making life more rewarding through improving your dealings with all the people in your life. If I could recommend only one book, this would be it. Read it, learn it, absorb it, apply it, and then carry on using it. It will teach you about persuasion, about letting people know that you're on their side in more effective ways. Combined with compound learning, it’s powerful stuff!

Whether you want to become a programmer, or the first woman on Mars, you’ll need the ability to find the little steps that'll get you there and keep applying them. Even if sometimes you get knocked backwards, if you keep applying the steps that compound interest, it will pay off. You will inspire other people and it will make you a better person. Win, WIN! The one thing I can guarantee is that if you do that, when you look back in ten years’ time, you'll go, “Wow! I don't recognise the person I was then and the person I am now.” I think that's the case with all of the most successful people in the world. They've all thought, “I want to be better than I am.”

One thing that's really important to me is to have gratitude for what you have *now* and to be kind to yourself. There is a flip side to being driven to be better; a trap that's easy to fall into. Don't let yourself miss today's blessings in your drive for tomorrow's or be unkind yourself if you don't achieve 100% of everything you want.

When you're being hard on yourself, imagine it's someone that you care about and say, "Would I do this to that person?" If the answer is no, you shouldn't do it to yourself either. Life is a journey (as is self-improvement) – you can choose to enjoy it, marvelling at how far you've come, or be constantly disheartened at how far ahead someone else might be. Enjoy your own journey and celebrate the successes of your fellow travellers. (If you're lucky, they might one day agree to be your mentors.)

Here's something I've learned about celebrating success and being happy. Your BIG aspirational goals are fine and dandy, even to be encouraged, but don't attach your happiness to them. Happiness is a current state of mind, not a future event. When you attach any portion of your happiness to future events, you lessen today's happiness. Not only for yourself, but often for those you love. Don't do that to yourself; you deserve better.

This year I got the opportunity to benefit 'go-giving' in a very direct way and practise both gratitude and being kind to myself. I was talking at an autism event on behalf of Titania, to say how we benefit from diversity in all its forms and how employing autistic team members has brought us great results. Before speaking at the event, I'd never met such a wide range of autistic people in one place. Without it, I may never have realised that I shared so many of their traits and challenges – or sought my own assessment. I guess you could say it's the perfect example of how 'go-giving' works: it's naturally reciprocal.

After 46 years, I'd just found out that *all my life* I've been autistic. For those who are wondering what autism is, the National Autistic Society says, "Autism is a lifelong, developmental disability that affects how a person communicates with and relates to other people, and how they experience the world around them."

When I got my diagnosis, my first thought was, "WOW – a disability. A lifelong developmental disability." It explained so many of the challenges I face daily, such as understanding why people 'beat around the bush', aren't direct, and don't just say what they mean. Struggling to understand how people sometimes say one thing but mean another and my lifelong obsession with studying social protocols and neuropsychology (I was filling in my natural deficit areas). It also explained why I find it completely impossible to work effectively in a noisy room and why I'm hypersensitive to light and scent. Suddenly, everything became clearer.

Looking back on my life, I realised this 'disability' has been one of my greatest blessings. It drove me to my first mentor, my grandfather, and his quiet room in our noisy house. It guided me to churches, where I met the people who inspired and supported me in my first steps towards self-development. It led me from the noise of the playground and its bullies to hide in the warm comfort of the coat rack with my cherished books. It gifted me with a mind that thinks outside the norm and comes up with solutions that are automatically 'outside the box', and, most of all, it made me who I am today. Autism is in my DNA, literally and figuratively.

My gift of autism, with all its challenges, has led me to today's 'happy ending'. I'm married to my true soulmate and co-own one of the most successful cyber security companies in the UK and have journeyed from 'council estate kid' to multi-millionaire.

I'm overwhelmed with immense gratitude for all that life has brought me and hope that my story will somehow inspire your own. If I can get here, then anybody can.

I'd like to wish you every success and leave you with three last things.

The first is those personal rules that have served me so well: 'Do good, forgive everyone (including yourself), and treat others as you'd like to be treated.'

The second is a little 'go-give' from Titania for those of you who are in a small business or charity of under 250 people. We've put some of our pro-level technology into an easy-to-use 'risk-assessment' tool. It will help you protect yourself against common but devastating cyber-attacks.

You can get it from here www.titania.com/risk-assessment-tool.

It takes less than 10 minutes to use and it's our gift to you – you can use it *for free*.

The third is to 'invest in yourself' – you deserve it and you never know where it might lead. Thank you.

HITHER MANN

"Business and making money is so easy compared with what I went through growing up. If you're mentally strong, you can achieve anything."

Job Title: Founder & CEO Fortune Academy

Personal Bio: Wealth Coach. International Speaker. Multiple Business Owner.

Business: Fortune Academy

Services: Wealth Coaching. Financial Trading Education. Public Company Listings.

Contact:

E: hither@fortuneacademy.co.uk

Website: https://www.fortuneacademy.co.uk

♦ ♦ ♦

I recall at the age of nine making a firm decision that I was going to be very, very rich. I didn't know how, but I was certain it was going to happen because I grew up in a family where lack of money was a major issue and there was a lot of arguing between my parents. I saw lots of aggression, anger, and sadness. So, as a simple child, I thought that money was the answer. Of course, it's not, but it was the thing that my dad kept preaching about.

We grew up with no money and I was taught in a traditional manner. Academic achievement was my passport to freedom, according to my dad. He told me that if you want to be wealthy, you have to do very well at school. So, I aced all my exams and studied really, really hard. I got an academic scholarship at a private school, which was a blessing because I think without that I wouldn't be where I am today in terms of having high standards. Of course, I didn't learn how to make money at school; they don't teach you that. But I certainly learnt high standards and I was around very wealthy kids. I didn't feel I fitted in at all during that period, so it made me even more determined to be like the other kids and have the family life that they did.

There were a lot of drivers around me, which was, I guess, a blessing in disguise. My first ever job, that allowed me to help my family financially, was at around 16 when I got a full-time job as a PA. I figured out which were the higher-paying jobs. I didn't want to do the temporary jobs, like working in a Tesco, because I knew they weren't going to pay that well.

So, I managed to get a higher-paid job and then three months later I went back to school. Every school holiday I was working; I never had a holiday as such. There were three sisters and I was the middle one. My dad treated me like a boy in the family. He didn't have a son, but he always reached out to me because he knew I was tougher mentally.

He kind of challenged me by saying things like, "Who's going to buy me a Mercedes when you're older?" And I just thought it was a normal thing to do – to make lots of money and buy your parents a house and cars. It got engrained at a very young age that this was the way life should be. So, my childhood was very much about striving just to move into the adult world and make money.

What was your career path after you left school?

I had academic qualifications in mind so I did an optometry degree, at Cardiff University. I enjoyed it for about four months, then I started to get bored with all the studying, but knew I had to finish the course. At the same time, I was hugely into martial arts, which I started at the age of 16. I did sports and I used to represent Warwickshire from the age of seven. That gave me a lot of discipline. It made me feel alive because I had so much trauma at home and I thought, “This is the only way I can tune out.”

I used sport as a vehicle to feel like I was winning. I had a fantastic martial arts teacher and he gave me massive discipline. I absolutely love Cardiff for that reason and I finished all my education and got a good degree because I had the kung-fu instructor as a great mentor and friend.

Then, straight away, I got a contractor job. I decided I would not follow the normal route of having an annual contract and an annual salary. I went into a temping job, whereby you get paid far more.

By this time, I was very good at selling myself because I’d learnt that from working my way up in little jobs here and there. I figured, “I don’t want to be doing these jobs all my life so I need to be very good at communicating with people.” So, I managed to get paid four times what average people would get paid, based on commission and sales and so on. I just approached it like a business; I was going to build my own network of opticians. But again, I got bored. I didn’t like the 9 to 5, or the industry for that matter – it all seemed unfulfilling.

I think I had deep-rooted anxiety from my childhood, which kept bringing up a whole rush of feeling very trapped. I felt very down.

I don't think anyone really grows up thinking, "I want to be an optician." It was very much the Asian culture which was suffocating me. I realised that I didn't pick this career and I didn't actually want to do it. I was only doing it for the money and because my parents picked that career for me, and that's the worst reason to do it.

Then a good friend from Cardiff sent me an email about a property networking group, saying, "You should go check this out." I was looking for any avenue out so I thought, "You know what? Property is something that everyone talks about." My dad used to show me *The Sunday Times Rich List* when I was ten and I remembered property was always in there. That was my simple understanding of wealth because it was mainly property.

I went straight into this networking group and I discovered the real gems in my life. I thought, "Oh my gosh, this is so different to school and university and everything I've been taught by my parents." I could really see a future in which I could build real wealth. I went crazy because I had a philosophy.

I hardly had any money. I was only three months into my career and thus I had nothing to lose. I went all out and negotiated some fantastic deals in property which were very 'below market value'. I borrowed from a rich guy to bridge the money, used a mortgage provider called 'Mortgage

Express' to do an instant re-finance at the full property value and the difference sat in my bank account as the 're-mortgage amount'.

It was fantastic, I was making £40,000 per house and I was doing three deals a week on average. Very quickly, my wealth grew. I don't know how I coped, but I had no friends my age because they didn't see things the same as me and they thought I was greedy. At 22, the division between me and my peer group was huge and I had to separate myself.

I always felt like I didn't fit in anyway, but eventually it became a huge divide and I was hanging out with people who were 20 years my senior who became very good mentors. I'd do the optician job in the day, and then in the evening my life would start. At 5pm, I would go to the houses, make appointments to see the owners, and start negotiating. I would carry on doing that, or be attending networking meetings, until 11.30pm, then I'd get to bed by about 1am and then wake up again at 6am to start all over again. I did that for years, but it gave me fantastic wealth.

Of course, my mental health was an absolute mess. But it was very liberating to be able to give my parents money. Some people surprise their parents and say, "Oh my gosh, I'm going to do something really nice for you: I'm going to buy you a house, I'm going to buy you a car." But I felt like I had to help them before I could build my own life. It was engrained in me. I felt I could fix things by throwing money at it. Well, of course, there's a lot more to it than that, as I learnt later. Money just gives slight gratification in the short term.

So, it has been quite a journey. I was happy, but it was very bittersweet because I felt very empty right up to the age of about 25. I'm 35 now. I bought my parents their house at around 23. I bought my dad a car for cash very shortly afterwards, which felt like quite a big achievement, but I always felt something was missing within me.

One thing I noticed was that people don't take you seriously at that age. Business owners, or business people, certainly underestimated me because they thought, "Oh, she's going to worry about breaking her nails." I was very much an unassuming character in meetings. They kind of laid their cards on the table by accident because they didn't think I was going to do anything with the information or be a competitor to them. It was not until I was 28 at least when people started putting up their guard and realising, "Oh, she is a bit of a threat. She can't really be told all the secrets that we used to tell her." Quite interesting.

But in spite of my financial success, I was very, very down and I had to think about having therapy. The first time I had counselling was when I was 25. My standards for my personal life were very low because of things I had witnessed in my childhood so I picked a boyfriend who reflected those beliefs. I was very upset, very fragile. Money and business were the only way I could express my freedom because my personal life was in such turmoil; that was the only way I could feel like a new person or feel reborn. I found business easy because the problems and the sharks I dealt with were nothing in comparison to my personal life at the time. I think that's why I was so tough because I had much more horrible things going on in my private life. So, the challenges became quite small. I was quite a tough character. Not much could break me, and it really paid off, in hindsight, when it came to business. But, of course, mentally I was in an absolute state; I wasn't happy at all.

The turning point came after I went to see my doctor and said, "I need medication. I'm getting suicidal." He said, "Nope. I'm not going to give you medication. I'm going to make you speak to a lady counsellor, she's fantastic." And I just thought, "Okay, I've got nothing to lose." She was my mum's age and she was from the same culture as my parents which was quite ground breaking. To hear her say things that were very different to what I was hearing at home made me feel like a new person. She told me, "A child will look for gratification from their parents." She realised I was just living for my parents by buying them everything. If they were not happy, I was not happy. I felt like the black sheep because I was very right-wing in my approach. I hated the Asian culture and I never wanted to date an Asian person because I didn't want to be like my parents.

My mum used to hate it when I said, "I don't care what other people think." She said, "You should always care what other people think." She only did things to impress people or to try to fit into a culture, and I found it suffocating. This whole cultural code I grew up with felt like an absolute shambles to me and I didn't want to be a part of it. So I had to step away. But in that process, I was very judged.

When that lady counsellor told me that an adult is someone who makes their own decisions and does not have to seek gratification from a parent, that was a changing point. That's when I realised, "Oh my gosh, I could end up like all these other Asian people I see, who are 50 or 60, and they are still like kids looking to please their uncles and aunts and parents." I decided then that I was going to be an adult. I knew it was going to create havoc, but I was going to stick to my own rules. Because I didn't see any reason I'd want to be like them. It was a long battle to get my own way and move out and live with a partner. That was very frowned upon and I lost all my family in the process. They are very judgmental, and they thought that money had got to my head. That was their way of dealing with it, I think.

Counselling was the biggest moment when I felt free; I realised money wasn't making me happy. It is a massive tool and it was the only reason I could stand up and speak out to my family. Before that, when I was 19 and did not have much money, I used to have the same mindset and hate all I saw. I'd think, "I don't want to be like you." But they used to mock me, saying, "You've got nothing to show for yourself. You're an absolute disgrace." They'd treat me like a failure. Only when I had money did they give me some sort of superficial respect. So, I realised the power money has. It gave me the power to say, "Well, I'm going to have my own house. And I'm going to leave. And I'm going to have my own partner. Whether you like it or not, this is the way it's going to be because doing things your way is not working for me." The process was such a lonely and depressing one that I realised how huge an uplifting effect my few sessions of counselling had. This made me realise that I too wanted to be the person who gave that beacon of hope to other people who had similar struggles.

I wanted to help bring people out of whatever anxiety they were going through. In 2008, I got into financial trading, very much by accident. I was 25 and had lots of money when the crash in the property market happened. I had lots of properties that were still very good value; they were still positive in equity and cashflow. But during this lull period, I was forced to stop and look at my life because there were no mortgages, no auctions, nothing was moving, so I had to stop. At that point I realised, "Okay, I can probably follow that ambition of becoming a life coach in order to help others."

But life had other plans for me. I got into financial trading because my mortgage broker did. He was a bit older than me, but my only true friend. He was the only person I could speak to. This guy was trading on the forex market and I saw a simple solution: "Wow, you can make money and not talk to anyone? I can escape my family and travel the world?" I hadn't been able to do this before because with property I had to be tied to the UK literally every day, and hand-hold every decision being made. Because firstly, I was a workaholic, and secondly, with property, if you do it at that level, you have to be around because you have to oversee the building being refurbed or being purchased, you have to oversee the contracts with your legal team, and so on. I was used to working very hard and not really enjoying my life, so I saw forex as an avenue to get a bit of freedom.

For nine months, I trialled forex for myself. I went on the Internet and googled 'How to trade forex.' I thought I'd mastered it, but this is where my ego let me down. I thought because I was good at property I would also be very good at forex, which was hugely naive. I lost about £350,000 in total over the nine months. I was devastated mentally since I didn't know how to master this industry through the Internet. I was on the brink of mental failure and defeat. What scared me the most was that I would be stuck in my old life with its sadness, not able to travel, not being free. This became my biggest driver because now I had attached freedom to financial trading and I really wanted to master it.

I discovered that the financial market was not like property networking groups, where you can go to one freely and meet people. You have to find the brokers, the in-between guys, that are dealing with the big banks and the big traders. So I approached a broker with a consortium of funds – £7.8 million – that I used to use to broker property into auction houses. This was not a normal broker, this was an institutional broker. I went to him because I wanted a proper trader, not an amateur, to teach me. So I gave him the money on the basis that he would introduce me to the top five guys in the City of London. Because I wanted to find these people but had no way to do so. They opened doors and I had a meeting with each one to find out which one I gelled with best. He was a tough character, but he was young and impressive. He came from a similar background to mine, where he had been brought up with no money. His life was like a movie – he had got rich very young and was living the high life and was pretty much a crazy trader in some ways, but I aspired to be like him. I loved the freedom he had. He became my mentor, though not instantly. He was a massive sceptic and he didn't actually want to teach me.

Traders are the most ruthless humans I had ever come across; they are a different breed. They're not like property people, they're not like business people, they're not like anything else. They are cut-throat, crazy people. Studies have shown that traders at that level and psychopaths have similar kinds of personality traits. Serial killers have the same make up mentally as a financial trader who's very successful. Who else can sit and comfortably watch millions of pounds wiped out in a day, or an instant, and not flinch? That emotional stability they've got is on par with a psychopath's and they can handle some crazy things. I realised straight away that I had my work cut out, but I was excited too. I'd seen enough madness in my life by this time and nothing really surprised me, including if people were horrible to me.

What he did at first was to try to mentally break me because he wanted to be sure I was up to it. He was happy to just take my money and trade it. He would have made me a lot more money, which was great, but what I wanted was to learn how to trade myself, and he was not keen to give out his secrets. When he realised I was still knocking on that door, he figured, "Right, let's see if she's tough enough for it. She thinks she's good, but let's see how good." So, he put me through mental trials, which seem quite funny looking back. He'd say, "If you're not here on time, to the minute, I'm leaving." He'd have this place that I would meet him – I lived two hours from London at the time – and I would get there at 6:02 perhaps, because of the Tube not running on sync, and he would disappear. Another time I had a meeting with him at 6.30pm and I met up with my friend Ed at 6pm at the same venue. I thought, "Right, we'll have a back-to-back meeting. When Ed leaves, then my trader will come." And that trader had a very strict rule that only I would be at the meetings, no one else. So when he saw me through the window speaking to Ed, he just turned around and left. He said, "I told you. You can't have any random people there."

What he was trying to do, in a nutshell, was to see how I dealt with setbacks and personal rejection. Because that's what trading is: dealing with setbacks, failure, to the level of your core, to the point where your ego is so bruised you are forced to question yourself. Your self-worth could get destroyed. In trading, you're going to lose more times than you win, but if you do your risk management in a specific way and you've got your head right, you will make a lot of money. I guess he didn't know about my childhood or my family life; rejection was something I dealt with on a daily basis, so I didn't break. A year and a half later, he gave me a couple of drinks. I was teetotal, usually; I never used to drink. He forced me to stop having green tea and ordered me a couple of cocktails because he had another test for me. He wanted to see me get a little bit tipsy – I think anyone would be who was "clean" normally. He had told me a lot of things about trading by this time, but there was one absolutely golden gem that I wanted to learn that he was holding back about allocation rules and how you hedge your portfolio. It's very technical, but it was like the Holy Grail. This is why some hedge funds are so successful through the 'bad' economic times, because of this set of rules. And he revealed it to me when I was tipsy. He told me, "Oh yeah, by the way, that thing you wanted to learn about hedging ..." He wanted to feel that he had told me what I wanted to hear, but was perhaps hoping that I wouldn't be able to take it in. But I found that fighter in me, and all that discipline, I found that sober spot. He gave me a test of three different portfolios. He was like, "Right, do it for this, this, and this currently." And I did. Then he said, "You know what, I need to give you more credit. I know traders in the City who've not been able to do this for eight years and you've just done it in one go." That was the turning point because he realised I really had the intelligence and tenacity for this incredibly tough industry and at that point onwards, he took me under his wing. He had pushed me to the point where I was supposed to break, like a normal human being, but I didn't. He had had his doubts about me because I was a woman. In our society we think of Wall Street and we just see men in suits. It's a cultural thing; it's not that females can't do it, they just don't see it as the norm. But in my family, I grew up like a boy, pretty much, so when I grew up, it made me strive in male-only or male-dominated environments.

All the things that had been bad in my childhood and my personal life became the biggest saving points for me eventually. Business and making money is so easy compared with what I went through growing up. I figured out that if you're mentally strong, you can achieve anything.

The biggest transformation for me has been having therapy and realising that life doesn't have to be the way people say it's supposed to be. Society and cultural pressures are actually a massive hindrance; they don't help people any more. It has been found that the most unhappy and depressed females are Asian females. Many women of my mum's generation live to please other people all their lives and they've never really figured out who they are. So, when their kids are married off, or they haven't got a purpose as a mum any more, they feel hollow. They've never been taught to think for themselves. That was a major transformation for me: breaking away from the culture and realising I could make my own path. It's been a lonely journey and initially I met a lot of resistance.

This is where Fortune Academy has been my biggest saving point. I now have a coach, a guy in Knightsbridge who charges a lot, who will say, "Right, we need to work on this." He makes me meet some of the people he deals with; they're doing contracts of £17 billion and they're ridiculously wealthy, yet they still get anxiety and have family issues. It is really good to see that it's not something to be frowned upon or brushed under the carpet.

If I was to offer other women advice, I would tell them that if you've really found that passion in your work, so much so that it is a direct reflection of you and what you stand for in life, you will more than likely be obsessed with it. In that situation, you can't really get balance. I think the only balance possible is knowing who *not* to have in your life – don't try to please people who are not supportive to you. I've had to make very cut-throat decisions and distance myself from family members who I felt were negative and toxic. Having that realisation was very empowering. Who you work with or who you have around you are the most important things for keeping very focused on where you want to go.

I reverse-engineered my life; I started with the end in mind. I thought, "When I die what is it that people are going to be remembering?" I don't want to be remembered as, "Oh, she had loads of money, but she didn't help anyone and she was miserable." I decided I was going to help as many people as I can because I can't take the money with me. I'm never going to deny that money is important and I'm going to show people how to have that kind of wealth. They don't need millions, but they need enough not to worry about it.

When I was 18, a good friend of mine said, "Oh, you should read this book. It's called 'An Inspirational Leader'." And instantly I thought, "Wow, what a person that would be! Amazing." I've never found the book. But those two words stuck and I thought, "That's the kind of person I need to be." I was a very introverted person, I never was someone who'd speak out. I was a very shy, meek character – I never dreamt of speaking in public. I only started doing it as soon as I turned 30, and only after I had a very clear understanding of where I wanted to go in life.

I saw other people talking on stage, inspiring others, and I thought, "My gosh, as much as this makes me want to die, I have to do it." Because I can reach more people than if I do it one-to-one. Friends and acquaintances used to reach out to me and say, "Oh, I've got a problem here. Can you help me?"

They used to see me as that beacon of light so I was helping them on a very small scale. But to expand that to people I had never met before, I had to put myself in a position where I was an influencer. Today, that means you have to have a social media account and be really active on it. You have to be a speaker if you can; speaking is really powerful because it gives you instant authority. If the message resonates with people, they will pay attention and listen. So I created Fortune Academy to give back as much as I can.

This month I'm setting up my charity for mental health awareness. I want more people feeling lonely and trapped to feel it's okay to seek support or at least find the tools to re-create their lives. It's going to be called The Fortune Family Foundation. I've created a platform on which I can build and really fulfil my legacy. I think you have to have a massive vision. One of my coaches was John Demartini and he said, "If you want to have a vision to change anyone's world, you need to have a vision as big as a city. If you want to change a city, you've got to have a vision as big as a country. If you want to change a country, you've got to have a vision as big as the world. If you want to change the world, you've got to have a vision as big as the universe." That really stuck with me and I thought, "Right, I have to do this in a huge way. I have to go all out and then people will come towards my message and they'll see hope and light."

I have students now who have been with me for three years and they have transformed immensely. My top female trader, she's incredible. She started with £10,000 three years ago on a credit card; now she's on £100,000. She's transformed as an individual, she's somebody else. At first, she was a very weak, fragile character. I mentor people the way I brought myself up through life. The strategy is one thing, but the mentorship is more about the individual. Usually I go into their family life: I figure out, for example, what their relationship is with their parents and with their partner. That is what I fix in my mentorship. I am being a life coach at the same time as giving them the money. My model at Fortune Academy is very simple: I offer lifetime education. People invest in the programme and they've got me for life and they've got Fortune Academy for as long as we're around – we hope to be around for a very long time – and they will get up-to-date information all the time on the programme they are enrolled onto. I will upgrade their knowledge; every time I see them I'll say, "Now that you've got through this hurdle and you've transformed, you're ready for the next level that can make you even better." Things they didn't even realise they could be better at, I will push them. That's my job.

Firstly, I love watching the transformation; it's probably the most fulfilling thing I've ever done in my life. Secondly, on a business level I will give them money so they make a lot more because I know money has got that power. So, I will give them a minimum £50,000 to £100,000. We will give people up to £2 million and they trade that on the financial market, then I take a profit split. They keep 25% of what they make, and I take 25%.

When people come to me and say, "I want to be wealthy," I actually make it quite difficult for them to enter my programme because I want to see if they've got what it takes – a bit like how my trader mentally tested me. I do it in a mild way though and I try to be very ethical. One of the questions I ask is, "What's the toughest thing you've done in your life?" One lady told me, "Oh, the toughest thing was I was the only female in an office full of men." She was very proud about that, but I said, "That's not going to do it. You have to be tougher than that." So I had to say no. The people I really love working with are the ones who have been broken and have put themselves back together. They went through hell in their lives and some have had much worse childhoods than I did. Others have had very easy childhoods. Unfortunately, those who have had an easy life will struggle because if they've always been winning all their lives, then trading is going to be the first thing that will teach them to fail. If they've really got what it takes, I will take them through that journey, but I particularly like working with tough individuals from the outset. So, I do have a filtering process. At my last event, a wealthy parent brought me his 17-year-old and asked me to teach him. I said, "I'd love to work with him, but he doesn't understand money or hard work. He doesn't understand the reality of life." I asked him to come back to me after he learnt how to make some 'hard-earned money', such as working from a supermarket, or whatever it takes for him to create his own money rather than rely on his parents' wealth.

It's a very tough industry. Professional traders are an elitist breed. They are not normal human beings, but they are very powerful. Once you're there, you can create wealth, you can do literally anything. You've got that Midas touch. I really love what I do, and I just want people to understand that hard work and being down and out are part of being successful. Being able to deal with the bad times will help you in the good times. So, let's help you to fix yourself first and then you can have whatever you want. It's a never-ending story, fixing yourself and building upon it, but one thing is for sure: the larger the obstacles you've overcome through life, the larger your successes will be in your future.

SARAH MCALLISTER

"I grasped every opportunity. If somebody called and wanted me to discuss Feng Shui on the radio, I did it even if I was nervous and sweating."

Job Title: Director

Personal Bio: Globe-trotting, nature-loving, classical Feng Shui master with a penchant for flying trapeze and soaking in hot tubs under the stars.

Business: The Feng Shui Agency Ltd

Services: Feng Shui consultation advice for homeowners and businesses and people designing new homes or renovations. Full architectural / interior design team available or can also work with client's appointed professionals. Chinese horoscopes for insights into your life and business. Auspicious date selection to plan important events and launches.

Contact:

E: sarah@fengshuiagency.com

T: 0844 848 4099

Website: www.fengshuiagency.com

♦ ♦ ♦

I fancied being in the diplomatic corps at one point while I was at school; I remember that because I was passionate about languages and I've always loved travelling. I was forever out of school, taking long holidays with my family around Easter time, but I always caught up quickly so it wasn't a problem.

It was idyllic in some ways: we travelled a lot and went to lots of beautiful places, mostly in the States because my father did a lot of business out there. But it was also bizarre, and lonely in a way, because Dad was always travelling and there were nine years between me and my sister so she didn't really want me hanging about. There were five years between me and my next brother so I was very much the baby. I'd say that it was a comfortable upbringing, but not one where emotions were particularly discussed and, being a natural empath who could 'see' energy, I was forever confused and would often remark, "it's the way you are saying what you say, not what you are saying". It used to drive my parents up the wall as they would reply with, "why can't you just take things at surface value?" My parents' generation were quite stiff upper lip.

I always had friends in different groups. I remember just doing my own thing and never feeling part of one group in particular. I wasn't a Goth and I wasn't just sporty and I wasn't intellectual, necessarily, although I had an aspect of that. I didn't really fit in anywhere, but on the whole, it was enjoyable. I did lots of sport, particularly netball – in fact, I had a few England trials for netball.

I was never very confident; that was the one thing that the teacher would point out. I had all the skill, but I never had the belief in myself. I went to a girls' grammar school and we were fortunate to live so close to such a good quality school.

I never aspired to go to public school because I saw it as a punishment – a cold, draughty place – and it was used as a threat in my household: "If you don't behave, we'll send you to boarding school!" I had no idea that it was considered by most of the rest of the world as socially advantageous. I found that out later in life when new acquaintances and boyfriends' mothers would ask, "so, what school did you go to?"

From about age 14, I worked quite a lot in my dad's company. He sold engineering products because he'd had an apprenticeship at Hoffman's before moving into travelling salesman-type jobs and eventually consultancy. I would do stock-checking and things like that: very basic outbound calls, maybe chasing orders or suppliers. I think he probably gave me the job just to keep me out of trouble. I also did work a lot at the local dairy, particularly in the school holidays, and university holidays as well, pulling pints of milk off the conveyor belt and stacking them in crates. It was absolutely mind-numbing.

To earn extra cash in the Sixth Form, I worked in a local pie factory as well, which was funny as we had to wear hair nets and white plastic boots. You had to be really, really hygienic, obviously. Then I did a stint testing grain samples somewhere in Worcestershire. A whole gang of friends did the same sort of jobs with me. Sometimes I temped at the dairy in the office, doing the basic secretarial work that you do as a youngster.

I studied German with European Business Studies to start with at university. I was a complete rebel there. I just went mad after having had quite a sheltered upbringing, didn't study much, and failed my exams and then my resits! Then I thought, "Okay, let's do German and French with Business Studies" because I just couldn't bear all the statistics and the computer programming. I was into literature and psychology:

I loved reading about Freud and the Viennese psychologists, and the French surrealists. I managed to eventually pass my first year and then I just dropped Business Studies completely and did German and French. After having knuckled down and applied myself, I got a 2:1, which isn't too shabby.

What happened after you finished studying?

After university, I was temping and the plan was that I would join a friend and go travelling in Kenya, but that didn't work out in the end as my friend got arrested (he was innocent) in Nairobi before I had booked my flight! I was madly in love with a guy in Wales, who I had met during my time at the University of Swansea, so I thought, "Right, I can't go to Kenya, so I'll go back and become a poet."

Despite having been offered a full-time position by the company I was temping at, I left Worcestershire and signed on in Swansea, which was highly novel and felt sort of rebellious, and thought I'd make my living as a poet while being madly in love with this chap. That lasted for about six months and then I think my parents dangled a carrot. They invited me away on holiday to Palm Springs, California, and I got a taste of that sort of lifestyle again. Suddenly, I became a little bit more ambitious and moved to Bristol and got myself some more temp jobs. My boyfriend came with me, but found it hard to adjust, and I remember the feeling of my heart snapping in two when I told him I didn't think it would work out. It was one of those magical twin soul loves which didn't really survive in the world beyond our own container. I regretted it for many years, though, as we had definitely shared a profound love and he introduced me to the world of Taoist sexual healing and the concept of the guy recycling his sexual energy to lengthen performance – oh my God, the lovemaking was off-the-charts amaaaaaazing (my main regret!).

So, I made a new start in Bristol, which at the time I found so cosmopolitan, much to the quizzical delight of some housemates from London. I worked for an insurance company for three months, on their phones, but I found that lacking in meaning so I decided to do something that had some purpose.

I landed a job as a day-care worker for people with learning difficulties. I thought it would be people who literally had 'learning difficulties' and that I'd just be helping them with some basics. I had no idea what all this involved until my first day at work. I was truly shocked and a bit worried, but I found my feet and it taught me a lot. But after about six months I thought that, even though it had been an incredible experience looking after these people, it was time to move on. I reframed that experience by comparing it to the *Sozialdienst* schemes in Germany, where young people opt for either six months of volunteering or national service.

Then I was offered three jobs and ended up as a PA in a legal expenses insurance company – not really by design, but because they needed someone who spoke fluent German. Then, of course, I started to get a bit pigeon-holed into being a PA and didn't find it remotely satisfying. I stuck it for about two and a half years and then came a moment when I was in the Sinai Desert. I'd been invited to go there on a belly-dancing holiday because my mother, who was then 65, was part of a belly-dancing group. Dad wouldn't go with her so he wanted somebody to go and look after her. I can remember distinctly doing my Kung Fu on a rock at about 4:30 am in the Sinai Desert thinking, "Wow, what on earth am I doing with my life? There's a huge world out here to discover."

So, when I went back to Bristol, I finished my three-year Shiatsu Practitioner course and my first year of training in Feng Shui at the South West school and remember feeling absolutely saturated at that point and thinking, "I can't learn or absorb anything else. I just want to live. I want to experience life." I had also done a whole load of Shamanism courses and sweatlodges and Wilderness Philosophy and Wilderness Survival courses so when I sold the house, I just jettisoned everything and went off travelling to America, New Zealand, Australia, Hong Kong, China, Laos, Thailand, Cambodia, India, and then back. It was amazing.

Did you make your biggest decisions when you were travelling or when you got home?

It's difficult to say. There were several subtle aha moments rather than one big one. The reason I got involved with the Shiatsu was that university had been quite traumatic, with a series of personal tragedies that made me really deeply question who we are and what we're all about. I ended up moving into a bedsit at one point, instead of a house share, because I just wanted to be on my own. I spent a lot of my twenties and thirties deeply engaged in more spiritual pursuits, while other people were getting on in the material world. I've only been going about that over the past five years – in a way, I did things backwards.

I don't think you can really define spirituality, but it has to be balanced by material stability and financial security. I don't buy into the broke healer thing. Life has to be balanced and that's been one of the big challenges with running this type of business – knowing your value and charging substantial fees. Whereas other practitioners, who may not be as qualified as I am, or are coming from a different, more basic, style charge a lot less because their work is not as in-depth or they are carrying that 'spiritual' story. There's a false idea that spiritual means you have to give things away for free or low cost.

When was the first time you learned about Feng Shui?

The first time I learned about Feng Shui, I was about 14 and we were in Scottsdale in Arizona. I saw a book on Feng Shui in a shop window and thought, "I'm going to build Feng Shui hotels." It was a random thought and then it disappeared. To put this in context, my father was a judo teacher, so from the age of about four or five I was learning judo, and he had a huge respect for the philosophies of the Far East. He would do Tai Chi and he encouraged us to do karate as well so all the Far Eastern philosophy is part of my upbringing. I suppose I always knew I'd do something like this, but I didn't really take it seriously – I just went down the school/university path. When I was in Swansea, after I'd graduated and was thinking about what I wanted to do, I saw a pamphlet for the Devon School of Shiatsu and picked it up and read about energy meridians affecting our psychology and our emotions and decided there and then that's what I wanted to do. I signed up to the closer Bristol School of Shiatsu without having done the taster course. I'd read *Dice Man* (Luke Rhinehart's cult 1971 novel about a psychiatrist who begins making decisions about how to live based on throwing dice) and I was into making decisions that seemed completely guided by something beyond my rational evidence-orientated mind.

On my travels, I saw a lot of important Feng Shui sites – not just the Chinese ones – because I'd already understood that Feng Shui was about the earth and earth energy and is not just Chinese, although it came from that culture. When I was travelling in the Australian outback, I visited sacred sites and then I saw the limestone karst peaks of Southern China, which was incredibly inspiring given my knowledge of Feng Shui. When I got back to the UK, I felt as if I could hold Bristol in my hand and longed to experience the vastness of London. So, I clinched a hybrid-style job at Deutsche Bank in London, with a view to taking over the project manager role in Frankfurt that my supervisor had originally wanted me to do, but got too busy being PA to the department head. It ended up as simply a means to an end, not really a serious career move: literally, the first week I was there, I told my boss I needed certain times off to do my next Feng Shui course.

Up until 2002 I had studied mostly spiritual Feng Shui: the intuitive style, symbolism, nature spirits, and so forth, so I craved some of the more methodical style and started an incredible journey with The Imperial School of Feng Shui and Chinese Horoscopes. I received my Practitioner Diploma in 2004 and then went on to do a ton of advanced courses; I also went back to China, this time with Grand Master Chan, and had two weeks in the Hunan Province, right in the centre of the country, which isn't that touristy. We looked at Chairman Mao's grave, visited his childhood home, and found out about the impact that the graves of his ancestors had on him. It was a really interesting trip.

I've seen Feng Shui in many, many different environments: Germany, Sweden, the Fire Mountains in Lanzarote, the Highlands of Scotland, the Middle Eastern Desert Form, to name a few. It applies to whichever country you're in. Feng Shui is everywhere, basically.

What led you to leave your job and set up your own business? Were you dissatisfied or was it just your passion for Feng Shui?

It was both. I wasn't particularly happy at Deutsche Bank; I didn't really feel it was my calling and then an amazing opportunity came when there was a department restructure and I was offered either redundancy or a job on the trading floor as a researcher. In hindsight, I wish I had taken the researcher role, but I decided to take the three months' salary and give myself a head start. I was always going to work for myself eventually, but that just fast-tracked it a bit.

I left Deutsche Bank in 2003 and for the first three years I didn't really have a business and lived off savings. I was working as a Shiatsu practitioner and had one clinic in

Greenwich and another in North London. But in one of my first years I brought in something like £3,500 in Shiatsu fees and my room fees were £3,000. Honestly, I look back and wonder what I was thinking. But when you're creative and you have a vision, you just go full steam ahead without much thought for practicalities. I went through my savings and in 2007 I got a part-time job in a niche property company that sold French chateaux and manoirs, and this was a good move because it helped to balance things out. It wasn't until 2009, a full six years later, that I had really established the business and hit that hallowed six figures!

When you come from a big business background, like working for corporations, it's quite hard to think like a small business. Looking back, the advice I would give others is that I should have been a self-employed consultant for many, many more years. I shouldn't have bothered with the headache of having a limited company and all the rigmarole that goes with it. Having said that, I always had a big vision and wanted to be really business-like. I knew I wanted to distance myself from the archetypal cliché of the Feng Shui consultant who's wafting crystals around. Not that there's anything wrong with that, but at the time I just felt that every Feng Shui website had terrible purple dragons or something awful.

When I had my last website done, I decided I wanted it to reflect more the kind of interior design and architectural collaboration work that we do. I'm really passionate about bringing the two worlds together; I always have been. I think that a lot of spiritual healers rub people up the wrong way because they don't want to even try to talk the existing language. If you're going to try and move society forward as a whole, you need to be able to talk the language of the masses to get your message across. I think that the more bridges you can build between the material and spiritual the better because you need it all to be balanced. I cringe when I see people charge £200 for three days' work. I just think, "Come on!" There's a whole industry that is undercharging and that's why a lot of Feng Shui consultants are hobbyists. They generally either have a husband/wife with a 'proper' job or just do a few consultations a year. I don't know anybody apart from the guys in the Far East (where obviously they have the cultural buy-in) who's doing roaringly well. Generally, most consultants are supplementing what they do by creating products or teaching.

What was it like in the early days of your business and how did it evolve?

I wasn't really marketing savvy. I was really chuffed when I first hit six figures. How did I get there? I think I had a bit of a wake-up call in 2007. I'd gone to New Zealand and I was engaged to be married and it didn't work out. When I came back to the UK, it was a bit tricky because I'd given up my flat in London and I moved in with my folks for a little while. I was looking after my dad a bit, who had developed vascular dementia, so it worked well and I think that gave me a real chance to get under the hood of what it was that I was doing and really focus on it as a business.

I can remember listening to a lot of seminars and webinars. I signed up to Infusionsoft. I was a really early adopter and I was constantly on the Fusebox helpline. I was trying to start to bring methods to the business to communicate with my list quite regularly. I'd always had the presence of mind to look into search engine optimisation, so I was found quite easily by people for invitations to key consultations or speaking events, which was really good. But it was all very homespun. I did pay a few people in the States to help me. How effective they were I don't know, because we weren't tracking that information, but I think it was more of an internal shift. I remember being approached by Red Bull and I thought, "This is the lowest I'm doing it for" and I felt really clean and clear about that; really detached. I think often the biggest shifts in my business have come from an internal shift that has made me see things with greater clarity.

I started teaching Feng Shui as well in 2005, which I enjoyed. Like a lot of people, I started off with three people in the class and two of them were friends! I can remember putting out flyers all around Muswell Hill. I made all the usual mistakes, like spending stupid amounts on printed advertising without any clear call to action or compelling headline – most people thought it was an advert for a Chinese takeaway.

I wish I could define some kind of recipe, but it was a very chaotic organic growth. Word of mouth was important; I've been very, very fortunate to do a good job and be so passionate about my work and I think that's what enrols people. When I did a job, I did it very well and people had a great result. I can remember literally leaping for joy when this young boy managed to sleep better after we moved his bed and space cleared the house. Maybe there's a joy factor and a passion factor that just push you through. So, 2009 to 2012 were really strong years: I was still teaching and had full classes and I was doing successful Google Ads, newsletters, speaking opportunities, and press articles. I got a lot of press without using a PR agency. I chased down every opportunity. If somebody enquired, I'd ring them back within the hour. I was just so passionate and very rarely said no to anything, although that can bring a bit of a burn-out as well and it's very difficult to sustain.

I had a part-time virtual assistant PA for a while, which was really helpful as she did all the work relating to the students and other tasks. I wish I could put it down to a method, but it was really more that I grasped every opportunity. If somebody called and wanted me to discuss Feng Shui on the radio, I did it even if I was nervous and sweating. I think you just have to put yourself out there. Whenever PR has come up, I've never thought it's about me, but more that it's great free exposure for my company. I am actually quite shy and, despite my humorous nature, I can come across as super serious on video and have really had to learn presentation skills. The toughest part is finding a way to just be myself in all my various dimensions and express my humour without being irreverent! Honestly, it is still something I am working on.

What does your business do today?

It helps homeowners and homebuilders to create spaces that are healthy and beautiful and stylish. I work from the outside in, to make small changes or create entire landscaping plans to bring good energy towards the property. Increasingly, I am working with businesses, which is really good fun as they tend to have healthy budgets to work with and I also get to look into staff compatibility through Chinese horoscopes, which can be very insightful for people. I've been asked to design a factory from scratch up in Sheffield next year, as the client wants me to help him design his house first. One thing I love about my work is how varied the clients are. They come from all backgrounds and while most are British, many have Indian or Chinese descent and I love swapping notes about my travels to their ancestral countries. My work has taken me all over the world, for which I am hugely grateful. I have dined with diplomats and government ministers and was even flown by private jet to Dubai once to consult on a huge new-build project, but always remembered how my father taught me to be just as polite to the porters/waiters as I was to the more influential people I encountered.

I'm not teaching currently, but I've done the video footage for some online courses which is soon to be edited, along with the supporting documents. I love getting involved with eco projects. Whenever I do a consultation, I always suggest that people use eco-friendly paints. In 2009, we were the first company to order a sofa from Flexform covered in hemp, for one of my clients. We had to send over hemp samples for

Flexform to test whether they could fire-proof it and whether it was strong enough, and so on. Feng Shui is all about respecting the earth. A massive part of the philosophy is literally 'combining the human with heaven and earth': about respecting nature and trying to walk lightly on the earth. I'd like to slowly but surely infiltrate urban planning policy throughout the world, to make places healthier and more vibrant. I have so much urban planning Feng Shui research – it's probably my next book.

You have done Feng Shui for a 108-acre resort. How do you go about designing something that big?

I did it in collaboration with resort planners. They did the whole scheme and I massaged it to comply with Feng Shui. I even delighted the owner as my suggestions freed up space to create a few more plots, which increased his ROI. When there's a new build, I have free rein to say, "It really needs to look like this and you need to do this right from the start." Invariably, especially with massive commercial projects, there's already some kind of concept in place and it's just a question of me making sure that it can incorporate as much good Feng Shui as possible.

A lot of my colleagues were surprised I was going to work alone on a project that size, without an assistant or somebody to run it by, but I didn't need anyone. It wasn't arrogance; it was just that when you're really passionate about something, you grasp a vision very quickly and it doesn't seem difficult.

I have tried to get my Chinese Feng Shui teacher involved with several projects over the years, especially with the

London Chinatown one, but he won't work with people that his horoscope can't 'combine with' and apparently his horoscope doesn't combine with mine! That saddened me as I really wanted a proper mentor in him. There was really nobody else to ask so I thought I might as well just do it myself and I felt confident taking that on.

You've worked on offices in Tokyo, a holiday home in South Africa, a hotel in Antigua. How does it feel to have your work all over the world?

Sometimes, when I read my testimonials, I stop and think about who's been positively impacted by my work and that's a really nice feeling. Travel suits my horoscope, you see, although it doesn't suit everybody. Some people are happier and better suited to doing local things and there's no judgement either way. My horoscope has lots of water, which loves to travel. I was in a 'follow water' phase at the time when I was travelling a lot and visiting about eight countries a year. These days it's not as active because I've moved into a slightly different horoscope state, which is more earth related.

I still love travelling, but I haven't been abroad as much. In the last couple of years, I've been to Copenhagen, Switzerland, and to the States a couple of times for some big jobs. And I might be going back to Japan because the company I worked for has expanded and they're thinking of finding new offices.

Your clients include Red Bull, Alibaba, Smiley, Sky Sports – why do you think they come to you rather than your competitors?

The key feedback I've had from people over the years is that I present myself and my work very professionally so maybe that's got something to do with it. I don't present a 'flashing dragons' look. Maybe they feel more secure contacting me because I'm not positioning myself as a spiritual 'walk on water' person.

I'm transparent about my qualifications and who I've trained with. I don't understand why a lot of consultants will write on their website, "I've trained with several Feng Shui masters", but never say who, or how long for. I think it's critically important to have a very clear CV.

Do you use mainly online or offline marketing?

It's a mixture, although it's only recently that I've started doing talks again. It took me about three years to fully recover from some really abusive so-called business mentors and during that time I was just too frightened to raise my profile because I didn't want to draw attention to myself. It was a horrible experience. I haven't done Google Ads for about seven years. I think business clients find my details online and then occasionally businesses refer me to each other as well, but the residential work is 90% word of mouth, which is hugely encouraging.

At many low points in business, where I have repeatedly struggled with mild depression, the fact I have helped so many people and they have referred me has kept me going. I used to get upset if somebody made a cynical statement, but because I've had so many great testimonials and referrals I've become immune to all that now. On the very rare occasion I have had a 'difficult' client (we've all had them), it has been so helpful to remember that a lot of my work is also repeat business (I keep track of this). I know from EXPERIENCE that Feng Shui works whether people believe in it or not, which could be a piece of useful advice to people in similar industries, whether it's Feng Shui or Reiki or crystal healing or something else deemed a little 'woo-woo'. You need that kind of self-belief when you're doing something against the mainstream. It's definitely getting better now: people are much more open than they were even three or four years ago.

I've gone to all those networking meetings. I was a member of Business Network International (BNI) for two years, in Hampstead and Highgate, and that might have helped a little in terms of getting my name out there. There was a lot of smirking and people saying things like, "Oh, do you make a living from that?" and "Oh, do you really believe it?" People smirk a lot about Feng Shui. Some people put you on a pedestal and think you're some sort of spiritually superior being – which I hate – or they'll belittle it. Happily, most of my clients are more level-headed, probably because I am a pretty balanced person and I never make wild claims like many consultants do. When I was starting out there was a lot of derision. Even now when I do radio interviews on TalkSport, they'll be talking about the Feng Shui of a football stadium or whatever with a tongue-in-cheek attitude. I've often wished I'd been a lawyer or something. I've had so many dinner party conversations when someone asks me what I do and even when I enunciate it really clearly, they still say "A *what*?!" It's still considered a little peculiar in some circles.

What have been your biggest obstacles and challenges?

Earlier on, people's cynicism did impact my self-belief at times, but then I kept on seeing the proof of the pudding and got over that hurdle. The biggest challenges as a small business for me were trying to find people to help me implement my vision of what can be done – graphic designers, website people, even accountants. To get all the ideas I have off the ground, I paid money to people and web-marketing companies (people who said they'll do my social media or SEO) and a lot of people just didn't perform well. The problem was, it was often money spent on a credit card that I could not afford not to see a return on. Apparently, this is a very female thing to do – plunge a lot of personal funds into a business, whereas men seek external capital. I spent far too much money trying to find people that I could move forward with in a meaningful way. I think that creating the right team is a massive challenge for small businesses. Delegating is much more of an art than I imagined it to be; I used to delegate tasks to people without having checked that they fully understood my instructions. You can't expect people to be mind readers, but you can't also be micro-managing either.

Managing finances has definitely been a huge lesson for me to learn and, having been advised to go bankrupt at one point, I thought, "OK, I really really really need to get this handled." Long term, my decision to hunker down and pay off debts was the right decision, but I have had many days where I think, "Oh, stuff this..." And the hardest thing emotionally to deal with is the pressure to have this perfect life. The Imposter Syndrome is worse when you have had amazing multiple six-figure years in business, then fallen down, and are rebuilding. It can be hard to move into the future while fixating on the 'golden years'. I cannot tell you the number of fails I have had! The number of disappointments. Huge projects coming towards me then literally evaporating. I really had to heal a lot of internal stuff around feeling like the universe was a 'wind-up merchant'! But then I would get busy again and when I am busy I LOVE what I do. I wouldn't want to do anything else.

One of the best insights I had was when I finally stopped internally bemoaning the setbacks and in addition giving myself a hard time(!) and became grateful for them and the opportunities they presented to re-set, re-align, etc. It is so important to understand that setbacks are simply part of life and not necessarily some message from the universe that you are on the wrong path. Get good at recovering from or, ideally, evading the setbacks that you can foresee and just keep moving forward, whether by inches or stratospheric bounds!

What is your experience of working in male-dominated fields like real estate and architecture?

Feng Shui teachers tend to predominantly be male and the students are definitely predominantly female, which leads to consultants being predominantly female. Obviously, there are male consultants as well, but far more are women. In architecture it's completely different and I've had several male architects hit on me. I've been saying, "Let's collaborate on a project" and it became clear that they were expecting something in return from me, which is highly inappropriate. I've had sleazy comments like, "Oh, so if you could Feng Shui my bedroom." After I've stood up and given a professional lecture at a RIBA sponsored event, that's all they can say to me! Another guy said to me, "Honestly, you're so brave – I take my hat off to you for talking about a subject like Feng Shui at an event like this."

The 'long shot' has been my specialism – almost an addiction. I wanted to revolutionise a staid industry. It's only recently that I've been focusing more on the places where people are raising their hands – before that, it was a little like me saying "I'm going to *make* you raise your hand" because I've been trying to focus on the mainstream rather than getting coverage in things like *Spirit and Destiny*, although I did have a stall once at the Mind, Body, Spirit Festival in 2006.

Generally, the work is client-led, so it's the client who wants the Feng Shui, not the architect. So, I face a lot of resistance from them and sometimes the client has no idea that the architect isn't listening to me. I have to then either sort it out myself or suggest – discreetly, because I don't want to whistle blow on the architect – that the client and I have a meeting with the architect and reinforce the importance of the Feng Shui. It can be seen as competitive: these architects have a strong vision and I sometimes disagree with that, which they see as a challenge.

Not all architects are like that. Some have been very collaborative and I've learned a lot from working with them. I really enjoy it. I've done a few small renovations and gutted a few properties under my own brand with my own building team and I'd like to do more projects like this with trusted associates because it is easier for my Feng Shui clients to have me and a project manager oversee everything.

What I enjoyed about full project management in the past was the products procurement and interiors sourcing, etc. and the fact it lets me be involved with something that's a bit more 'real world' (and therefore more profitable) because Feng Shui is mostly so intangible. I can only rely on anecdotal testimonials. It's very difficult to measure its effectiveness although there are quantum science experiments being done now, measuring the space before and after in terms of quantum molecular activity and so on, particularly when it comes to water.

There's also research done about people's brainwaves when they're in a good Feng Shui space and when they're in a bad Feng Shui space. So, I'd like to move more fully into the architecture and design arena and have employees, as currently there are just associates – which has been lovely and flexible, and gives a lifestyle business, but I feel like more of a challenge coming on. I just think that an evolution would creatively satisfy me and be business savvy as well.

What are your major aha moments over the years? What keeps you getting out of bed in the morning?

I had a revelation a couple of years ago. I was meditating on the multi-faceted nature of the world and the sheer abundance of this planet.

You know when something's deeply profound and meaningful to you but might not necessarily translate to other people.

I found myself really tapped in to the true abundance of the universe. If you think about how many leaves there are or how many drops of rain or how many atoms of air, it's mind-blowing. I experienced such a deep sense of joy and fundamental truth that it made me laugh out loud.

I am also encouraged by the fact that I regularly see new patterns in the theory and new ways of applying Feng Shui and Chinese horoscope techniques that no one has taught me exactly, but that make logical sense. It's truly inspiring. And because of my deep understanding of chi from my Shiatsu training, I know that it isn't delusional.

I am always learning in one form or another and I regularly review notes from advanced classes as there is so much precious material in them to practise and get it into the muscle, so to speak.

How do you cope with cynicism from others and your own self-doubt? How do you find the strength to carry on and ignore it?

One thing that I found really helpful was to really, really commit to following my bliss. Last year, I took up flying trapeze again. I had done it for around six months when I was living in London in 2006 and I loved it. I took it up again last March until September then had a break and I have just started it again. I also did static trapeze to build up my upper body strength and I've been doing a bit of adult gymnastics locally. It's so empowering because the circus is all about people of different shapes, sizes, and backgrounds coming together. That's one of the core principles of the circus. It never felt like I was over the hill or a delusional person who fancied themselves as a trapeze artist. The circus people understood that it was about joy. There's nothing like it. I absolutely love it. It's frightening, it's scary, but it's also so empowering when you get it right and you get to that moment where the fly is co-ordinated. There's that moment in time when you're just leaping through space before the catcher catches you. It's amazing!

Challenging myself to do things that are slightly difficult is important. For example, I didn't have much upper body strength. I think my first class at the circus I tried to get up a rope and ended up crying – in the toilets, not in front of anybody – because I felt so puny. But the more you do it, the more you develop the body strength.

Being immersed in nature is key to my equilibrium and wherever I've lived, I've always made time to take a walk and meditate or sit under a tree or something similar. Nature has always made sense to me, even when I was a kid. In fact, it was highly instrumental in my healing from the problems at university because I did a lot of wilderness survival training in Sussex, which was amazing. What I love about nature is that it's not like a guru or a prescriptive process; it lets you unfold and just be. It doesn't push you into anything. It doesn't tell you a certain way of being. I think that's what is so powerfully reassuring about it.

If I am feeling scattered, I also really love to do a yoga session – at home, usually, as I prefer going at my own tempo. I love how yoga simultaneously brings me back into my body while also freeing my mind. I also love to do Sacred Silence meditations in nature as these help me to connect with the universe and re-energise my light body. I find that Chi Kung turns me into an insomniac so I far prefer homespun yoga and, having been on two full-on yoga retreats, one in Devon and one in India, I know sufficient to know what I am doing.

Keeping your internal vision is also key. I have a vision board and when I remember to look at it, it's very powerful. I am also, now, much more aware of my emotions and regularly have Rosen Method treatments from an amazing 83-year-young practitioner. He is like a healing wizard. I also try to have acupuncture seasonally, too, as that is always worth doing, but I like also not to be too rigid and move towards what feels right at the time.

What advice do you have for others wanting to achieve what you've achieved?

Just have a genuine passion for what you do. I think we mentioned it earlier: don't be afraid to challenge yourself. Don't be afraid to put yourself out there. Do talks; engage with the media and so forth because I think a lot of people are afraid of doing that.

I think people hold back sometimes. Some really skilled friends of mine won't do a consult because they're too frightened – they think that they'll get it wrong – so a lot of people remain hobbyists. My second Feng Shui teacher was great. She said, "As long as you've got a benevolent intent, it'll all work out fine. The universe will never give you something that you can't handle." A lot of theorists in my subject have endless debates about this, that, and the other and then just have two consultations in a year. Everybody has to start somewhere. Even the grand masters started somewhere.

It's important to be a self-starter, as well. Again, it's that passion that makes you tenacious and gives you the energy to follow through. There've been some opportunities that I attracted and then didn't follow up on (then tortured myself about!), but I've chased down most of them. You have to create your own luck, which is saying something considering I'm a Feng Shui consultant. Again, it comes back to balancing the spiritual and energetic with the material. It's not enough to have the vision – you have to find a way to implement it and take timely action, but without being too calculated about it. That applies to anything, I think, and any person doing what they're doing. We need to find that middle ground between spontaneity and practicality, if it even exists; or maybe go off and be spontaneous in some moments and then more practical at others. I didn't get handed opportunities or connections from a well-connected daddy or husband – what I have achieved so far has very much been down to my own ingenuity, vision, passion, and tenacity. Well, that and a fair few Feng Shui water features, auspicious date selections, and obsessing about the precise compass orientation of my desk...

GEETA SIDHU-ROBB

"I've never forgotten how it felt when I was homeless, I had little money, and I had £14 a day to feed four people.

Job Title: CEO/Director, Nosh Detox Ltd

Personal Bio: Experienced leader, author, and motivational speaker. Founded and grew the Nosh group of companies from the start-up phase to a multi-million-dollar entity. Developed and branded the leading market product range of Raw juices. Created joint ventures with other brands in the industry, including Harvey Nichols, Quintessentially, and Wall Street Journal.

Business: Nosh Detox Delivery Ltd, Nosh Infusions Ltd, Nosh Raw Ltd

Services: Detox. Juice Fast Diet. Delivery. Wellness Centre. Coaching.

Awards:

2017: 'Champion of Innovation', Champion of Women Awards – The Dovetail Agency
2017: 'Entrepreneur of the Year' – London Asian Business Awards
2016: 'Healthy Food & Drink Award' (Silver) – Health & Fitness Magazine
2015: 'Healthy Food & Drink Award' (Silver) – Health & Fitness Magazine
2015: 'Best Health Supplement–Winner' Nosh Raw Booster– Beauty Shortlist
2015: 'Best Healthy Food Bar - Runner Up' Nosh Raw Energy Bar – Beauty Shortlist
2014: FDIN 'Innovation in Packaging Award' – Nosh Detox
2014: 'Businesswomen of the Year' – Geeta Sidhu-Robb – The Sikh Awards

2014: 'Best New Health Food or Beverage Award' – Finalist – Gulffood
2013: 'Best Innovative Beverage Concept' – Finalist – DrinkTec
2012: 'Innovative Health Product of the Year' – Silver – The Raw Smoothie
2011: 'Employer of the Year' – British Asian HAFTA Award
2011: 'Businesswoman of the Year' – World Sikh Awards
2011: 'Best Detox in London' – Evening Standard Magazine
2010: 'Entrepreneur of the Year' – Geeta Sidhu-Robb – Precious Awards
2009: 'Best Diet Delivery' – *Zest Magazine*
2008: 'Best Detox' – *Vogue Magazine*

Contact:

E: info@noshdetox.com

T: 0203 697 1366.

Website: www.noshdetox.com

♦ ♦ ♦

I grew up in Malawi, in Central Africa. It's a small landlocked country, including a lake which takes up one third of the area. Unfortunately, it's currently one of the five poorest countries in the world, which is sad. But growing up, it was, on some levels, completely idyllic. We had a big garden: farm, animals, nature. It was 100% in the middle of nowhere. I'm an introvert because I grew up, in essence, completely on my own. The flip side of that was that I was a bookworm. I read everything in my whole house, including all the "Reader's Digest" manuals, by the time I was about 12.

We didn't have TV so we grew up without any outside stimulation. So, I'm capable of spending enormous amounts of time in my head, which is not always a good thing! It was my parents, my brother, and myself – and a couple of dogs, a couple of cats, and the odd chicken.

I grew up in what was about four steps away from Apartheid. We grew up as immigrants in a society run by black people and funded by white people; it meant that we didn't fit in anywhere. So it felt very much like we were the Jews of Africa – I heard that as a phrase when I grew older and I was like, "Exactly! That's what it was." We were allowed to do trade, we were allowed to make money, and allowed to do all sorts of things, but it was as if we were forbidden to ever fit into the mainstream.

I remember, at five, going to this convent that all the Indian/Asian girls were meant to go to and thinking, "I hate this. I really don't want to be here." I said to my father, "I want to move." My brother was already in another school and in those days, you got educated – and in my background, which is sort of wealthy, upper-class – you educated the boys the best, but you always educated girls. You didn't not educate them, because they were eventually going to run something with somebody when they married, so you always had this dichotomy. I, on the other hand, wanted to get into what was, in essence, the white school – the western, British colonial school. They told me, "Well, you can't. It's for ex-pats." And my father was like, "What do you mean, she can't? Of course she can." My father was a brilliant feminist, but that didn't stop them from putting me through this battery of tests. I remember having to answer hundreds of words in spelling tests: things like 'generous' and 'island' – words no five-year-old knows.

Luckily, I'm a bookworm and learned words constantly – that was all I did. I learned how to read when I was about two, and just loved it and did nothing else, so I passed those tests with flying colours. I got one word wrong, and I always remember I called it 'izland' instead of 'island'. Then I set forth to become a troublemaker because I thought, "How dare you not want me? How dare you not let me in?" I think that survivor streak was born in me very young. That's what school was like for me. We lived with discrimination, racism, as part of our everyday fabric. There were clubs we weren't allowed to go into because we weren't white. You'd need to have a white person come in with you and take you back in. If you were allowed membership there, it was because you were a superior brown. The discrimination went all the way through school. So I always had to be best.

After primary school, I went to high school and then the discrimination became worse because all my western friends were starting to date and hang out. There were 10 different nationalities in my classroom, including Greek, Cypriot, Thai, Pakistani, Indian, and American. We got to the stage where at home it was "study, study, study" and then I'd go to school, and it was always, "God, you're really weird. You never come out." When my western friends started going out, I just had to stop being friends with them because I couldn't be part of that community because my cultural community wouldn't allow me to do that. That was a real trauma and so I became weirder.

I started acting because I loved it and it made the negative aspects all go away for a while. Back then, politically, we lived in a very dangerous society because we were a dictatorship. We'd wake up one morning and the father of the person sitting next to us would have had an unexpected car crash. He also just happened to be a member of the political opposition – and that happened two or three times during my years in high school.

We lived under huge amounts of permanent stress and danger. Then, the government nationalized all of the lands outside of town. My father had a huge tobacco farm and it was taken away because we weren't black. So he had to start all over again. This was a very tense time and I remember thinking, "How are we going to survive? What are we going to do to make money?" My brother was already in England: the exchange rate was 20 to 1, so if you spent £1, you had to make 20 kwacha. It was very tough. That happened two more times before we finished school. We were always pivoting and fixing and working. It was resilience, I think, that got us through. It was a very different upbringing, and it's very funny because I always look around now and I see where we are. I'm looking out on this beautiful square in Chelsea, in King's Road, in a beautiful townhouse – in my nice pretty dress. It couldn't be more different.

I came out to school here in the UK on my fifteenth birthday because I think my mother figured that dating was going to start and she didn't want me to do it at home because I was going to cause chaos; I wasn't somebody who liked being told what to do. She took the opinion that if I was out of sight and out of mind, it might be better for the reputation of my family. But looking back, I think my parents also wanted us to have best education we could which, in those days, was in the UK.

I did not have a great transition period with this because I grew up very much alone. It wasn't that I was lonely; I didn't know any better. I was quite happy with my own company. I was thrust into a state school here, with people who didn't like my accent and who were having sex when they were very young – all the stereotypes from an inner city. I just didn't fit in at all and I got bullied. So, I started to dumb down. I was too good at school because I'd come through this amazing private school system – the colonial school system was amazing. We grew up extremely wealthy, so we walked out from this lovely, privileged, but quite a difficult background - we weren't really spoiled, but we were very privileged. You can't really get spoiled when your whole ethos of survival was tested on a day-to-day basis. I went to boarding school for my A-levels, and that was nice because it was a Quaker school. It was a smaller community of people. I still struggled because I didn't fit in, I didn't know how to fit in, and I didn't understand people my age. I think that's just because I didn't grow up with people around me, and I looked around and thought, "What are you doing and why are you doing it? Why do you get drunk? Why do you smoke? Why do you do all these things?" I probably just had a very active inner mind.

My transition here was so hard simply because we grew up so differently – it wasn't only from being brown. That was really tough. It started to look up when I left school because then I went to university. I enjoyed university though I found it very hard to make friends because, for me, it was always difficult to find people to relate to. I did have friends, but not people where I felt that connection. At home, we had all gone through the same thing and it gave us this enormous connectivity. I did make two deeply good friends at university and I started to date. I think back to when I came here on my own: I didn't know how to get a job. I didn't know people here. I didn't know anything and I came out to law school. I got married very young because I was trying to make a home. I think I met my ex-husband when I was about 21 and then married him at 24. I just wanted to not be alone in this hostile place.

I actually got my first job as a lawyer through an introduction from a friend. From there, I worked in law in different areas for about 15 years until I started my business, Nosh. So I got my first job through an introduction and then I worked in corporate law. I did a Master's in International Finance at the London School of Economics. Then, that led me to some other more interesting work. I never really wanted to be a lawyer, though. I was only a lawyer because my father wanted me to be one. It was that or a doctor, and I thought, "Shoot me now, I'm never being a doctor." Look what I do for a living now; isn't it funny?

The defining moment for me, when my life changed, was when my first child was allergic to his vaccinations, so he was ill. He spent about 230 days in hospital in his first year. He got, in quick succession, eczema, then that went into remission, then asthma, and then he got anaphylaxis. I remember he had sliced turkey, pressed with cold milk. In those days, there weren't regulations about this, no food description or labelling. We were in the hospital and he'd had an anaphylactic reaction. They were trying to put an IV line in him. I was holding him saying, "Don't struggle, don't struggle." He stopped moving and it was Code Blue – his heart stopped beating. They had to resuscitate him and he spent a week in intensive care. He was tiny – barely a year old. And he had all these tubes sticking out of his body.

I looked at him when we were sitting in the recovery room they put us in after he was released from intensive care. I thought, "Do you know what? You guys do not know what you're doing and you will just mess this up." Everything the doctors told me to do was wrong. Everything. I said, "Should I get him vaccinated?" They said, "Yes. If it were my child, I would." I knew it was the wrong thing to do because I'd done my research – being a lawyer, the only skillsets I had were reading lots of information and pulling out details that were relevant. Then they said to do this, then they said to do that. Then they wanted to give him the MMR jab, and that was a huge battle with the medical profession because they said, "You'll go home from hospital, and we'll give him an MMR when you're not here." I responded, "You haven't got the right to do that." Every time he was in the hospital, I'd sleep on the floor and I would never leave him. I thought, "Sod it. I am absolutely doing this my way. We are never coming back to a doctor." That was it. I still don't think I've got a registered doctor. Somebody asked me the other day who my doctor was, and I looked blankly at them and thought, "I don't know really – I haven't got one."

I drew on my upbringing for meal inspiration – healthy Asian food. We ate balanced meals. My mother was really into health food. My grandfather was a homeopath so my mother always used homeopathy. I was brought up to think and understand that there were other solutions and I just had to find them.

It was a seven-year journey of doing anything that would work. We would drink this Chinese brown, gunky, shitty tea. Acupuncture needles. I tried everything. My son went to see a healer and she was fantastic, so I thought, "Right, how do I become a healer?" I couldn't afford £100 per half an hour, or whatever it was. So I went into the healing course for a year and a half. Then yoga made a big difference, so I thought, "I'll just go learn how to do yoga." Everything that would work, I would learn how to do it because it worked on my child, and then I thought, "This poor boy. I'm going to end up smothering him my whole life," so I looked around and thought, "I must have more children." It's funny how very calculated a decision it was. I met this man, married him, and had two more kids and along the way, I cured my son's asthma and the eczema. When it came time to vaccinate my younger children, I refused. We fought vaccinations. During this time, I wrote and published a book on eating allergy-free as my son was allergic to dairy, gluten, fish, eggs, and nuts. It was really hard to feed him, and I knew other mothers were having this problem. The clinic we had would send people to me to help them to work out what to eat and how to eat.

I also started to speak publicly because there were just no people saying the things that I needed to hear, so I started saying them. I remember doing a speech one day; there were around 200 to 300 women in this room. It was a mothers and children asthma-type event – because back then, if mothers said, "I think it was caused by the vaccination," doctors would respond with, "Uh, women always say that." It never occurred to them we might be right. I thought, "You know what? I'm big and strong enough and loud enough that you're not going to shut me up," as everybody else was scared to say things.

After this, I ended up divorced again with three small children under the age of seven, and really without any money at all. We had about £200. My mother – my father had died – was very unhappy that I had left my husband so we were basically without any resources. I rang up a girlfriend and said, "We've got nowhere to sleep tonight." She said, "Come, come, come." So we slept there for a few days because I had no idea where to go with three small kids, no money, nothing.

She gave us somewhere to stay: my kids slept on her bed and I slept on the floor. I thought we'd only be staying there for a week. But it took a bit longer than I expected. It was a very hostile divorce, from which I got absolutely no money, so I thought, "How will I make enough money to survive?" I couldn't rent a place and I was stuck. Thankfully, my girlfriend gave us somewhere to stay and we ended up there for six months. So many people along the way in my journey were kind, loving, supportive, and helpful. I gave her a huge number of shares in Nosh when it became worth something as a thank you, but that's not recompense, is it? It's love when somebody does that for you.

I think most people don't have the privilege of knowing what would happen to them when they have nothing, and their back is against the wall, and they're 100 per cent vulnerable. Most people don't know that about themselves or what would they do. I stood for parliament when my son was born. I'd been selected for a parliamentary seat for the Tories. I was the first brown woman to stand for parliament in this country. I had done a lot of TV in that one year while we were campaigning. My poor son used to get fed while sitting in the back seat of cars. I'd feed him and then go and stand up on stage and do a speech – it was really funny. He went canvassing and door-stepping with me too. When I had no money and I didn't know what to do. I didn't want to ask for more help and I thought no one would help because if my own family wouldn't help, who would? But I was lucky because a lot of my friends, who were lower down the ladder earlier in my life, now had their own shows on TV. I told them, "I'm really desperate for work." They responded positively. "Yay!" they said, and they gave me shows and that paid me £2,000 to £3,000 at a time. I did the most amazing TV stuff. I did a whole segment on immigration for Channel 4; I did speeches for money; I did just about anything for money. These lovely people really stepped up to help me – it really pays to be nice to other people, it pays to be decent as a human. They just all stepped forward and helped. One of my friends rang and said, "This guy's looking for someone to do this." That led to work for a year and a half and the guy paid me a fortune every month. One time, I found myself in the middle of Russia, negotiating to broker a deal between two separate parties as a corporate negotiator. I was getting paid huge amounts by the day and there were all these men with beards, guns, and me. That was a little terrifying.

I had somebody looking after the kids when I travelled. I spoke to them every day and thought, "Please don't die while I'm gone." I did a few of those jobs. I did another in Saudi Arabia and another one in Dubai. I sold licences for setting up telephone companies in Rwanda, Kenya, and Tanzania. So somebody would ask me, "Can you do this?" and I'd say just three words: "Yes. How much?" I'd fly in. I'd fix it. I'd fly back out and they'd pay me. They would sometimes say, "This is undoable." I would say, "So if I do it, will you give me more money?" They would say, "Yes." So I'd go off and do whatever it was. I don't think I failed once.

Then my goddaughter, who had lived with us for about five years, nominated me for Working Mother of the Year. So I went to 10 Downing Street to receive this lovely award.

Then my girlfriend came around while I was whining about being poor and she said, "Can you shut up about being poor? I'm fat." My best friend had two kids in one year and I said, "Oh, my god, don't be ridiculous. Just do this, this, this, this, and you'll be fine." I was giving her answers and then I went back to, "Can we talk about me being poor?" The kids were still in private school because the one thing I didn't want to change was their school environment though I had no other way to pay for it than working. I spent every penny on rent and school fees. I wore the same 10 outfits for nearly three years. There were a couple of days that were painful because I hadn't paid the fees on time and they'd handed my youngest child back to me through the school door saying, "Not until you've paid your fees." I had to lie to my child – I was like, "Sweetie, I thought you and I needed some time together." She asked, "Can I go back to school tomorrow?" I rang my mother in tears, but she was travelling and said she couldn't help. I even rang my ex that day. But he refused too. So, I went to a friend and I begged, "Please, please, please, I really need some money for these school fees." She gave me around £2,000 (which I did pay back). Everybody was asking, "Why don't you just take them out of private school?" I said, "No, I'm not going to."

I had said to my girlfriend, "Here's what you need to do to lose weight." Six weeks later, she rang me up and said, "Do this for a living. People will pay you money for this. I'll pay you money for this. You must do it!" So in 2007, I set up Nosh for one year as a beta test. I found a £2,000 overdraft that I hadn't used and begged the bank to resurrect it. They did, and I used £1,800 of it setting up the company and so we had to make a success of it because otherwise we'd be screwed. We started Nosh on the 6th January 2007 and ran it for that year. Then, in 2008, I started working it full-time. It has supported my children and me ever since.

We were working from my kitchen table at the start. I had one person working with me and she was my Operations Manager, who dealt with the kitchen stuff and everything else. I dealt with the rest of it, including sales and marketing. After that, we just got on and sold. We sold it to parents, we sold it to everybody. We couldn't afford PR, we just had to get inventive. So we built a referral, word-of-mouth business because we have a product that works. The goal was to never say no to a client. So if a client rang up and said, "This is my problem," our response was always, "How do we find a solution?"

That's how we came along. We created juice fasting in June 2008 and started delivering that. Juice fasting and home delivery didn't exist in this country. We were doing home delivery of gluten-free and dairy-free food. So it was easy to get a certain amount of attention, but then people would tell me, "You should be a nutritionist. Why aren't you one?" Ultimately, I did not want to go back to school. We rented a kitchen in Battersea and when we were about four years along, we borrowed money from the bank and built a kitchen. At the beginning, the goal was always to pay bills, pay bills, pay bills. But after about four years, I thought, "How do I grow this?" I really needed to learn how to run a business so I did an executive MBA at Cranfield Business School and worked out that I hated numbers with a passion. Then I wanted to learn how to market my business. There was a guy in L.A. who was teaching a course, and I wanted to learn from him. Initially, I didn't know how to do that. My girlfriend said to me, "It's a great opportunity. You're a corporate lawyer – I want to invest in your business." So she wrote me a cheque for £82,000.

I nearly passed out and it was a good thing I was sitting down. I took that money, and flew in and out of L.A. once a month for 13 months. I would literally fly in and out (11 hours each way!) for 2.5 days. Then I got clients in Hollywood as well; that's how we grew the business. Gwyneth Paltrow became a client of ours and started to recommend us, so we got other celebrity clients.

Being foreign, we found it really hard to get press in the traditional media, whereas the non-traditional media was easier. I made a list of every blogger in 2011 and sent them food, gifts, juice, etc. Some of them are really big these days, it's amazing, and our videos are still on their sites. They've never pulled them down. That's how we grew: we bootstrapped. Then I got a bit more funding in 2010 to 2012 because I wanted to put in software for the business. So, we put in an administrative system because to me that's an extra body that's actually helping me. That's how we grew more.

Then, in 2015, I thought I should do crowdfunding so I could have some money to open a shop. I didn't really understand the concept of investment. So I built our own crowdfunding platform. I thought, "This can't be that difficult, can it?" We took different bits of software that we were already using, read the financial statutes, wrote it up, and got a lawyer to look at it. It cost us £4,000 to build the whole thing and we raised £150,000 in four weeks.

It was a really good idea and we added credibility by showing who we were working with. For example, we were working with some people at KPMG at the time, who were lovely. They did this whole report on how big the Wellness Industry was and we published that in an email. We also sent out an email saying, "Why Blackrock loves Nosh" because a lady from Blackrock had invested in us, bless her. And one of our clients, who traditionally bought our stuff from Groupon, invested the most money. That's how we raised all the investment. Now we have about 20 per cent really solid famous household names as, alongside Gwyneth Paltrow, they all refer more of their colleagues.

At one point, we were putting our products in Waitrose. We had a whole retail arm going until Brexit, when the pound dropped 19 per cent. I suddenly found out that I was paying to put products on the shelf, because the margins were so low. I had a margin of 12 to 14 per cent, and it was costing me 19 per cent because we were importing stuff from Europe. We lost so much money in those couple of months, and I decided not to do it any more. So, I pulled everything out – I literally woke up one day and thought, "Right. My business will die if I don't do something." When I pulled it all out, people like Ocado were furious because we were the third-biggest-selling juice in Ocado. I said, "I'm so sorry. But we can't do this."

Then we took the opportunity to rethink the whole business plan. We had a clinic in Harvey Nichols for six months – a pop-up – but I didn't like working under somebody else's umbrella. So we moved to our own clinic. We had our own restaurant, which, again, was a pop-up. Again, we've moved to our own premises. We added on Health and Lifestyle coaching, which is one of the fastest-growing parts of the business. I brought infusions, or vitamin drips, to this country in 2013. My passion is now to open 15 clinics. I like the bit when I'm speaking to people; I like the business model based on events, conversations, and coaching. I love it when somebody walks through the door and I can say, "Right. Here you are, let me transform your life for you." Then you can be sent away with all the knowledge and skills you need to live a healthy life, but you can stay a client if you want to stay.

We're franchising now. We're looking at global franchises. We're talking to two or three countries. Now is the time to build Nosh because now my kids are older – my daughters both had scholarships at school and my son is at university.

Before this, it was just time to survive and keep a roof over our heads.

Right now, we do coaching, we do videos, and we do food. I was talking to somebody the other day and she was saying that luxurious experiences are really going to be where we go in the future, and I think health is the ultimate luxury. So I want to position ourselves as a global wellness brand. That's my vision: that's what would make me happy. I think the happier you are as an entrepreneur, the more successful your business is.

I have lightbulb moments every day, practically. Ultimately, it's such an internal journey. We think building a business is an external journey, but it isn't. So you create an environment that allows you to support yourself internally more than anything else. I have my rituals: I wake up in the morning, I meditate, and I work out. I'm very true to myself and I think that's so important. I won't do something that I don't believe in. We had somebody who said he really liked the ethos of Nosh, which was lovely but surprising. I hadn't thought about it because I'm not doing it for you to care about my ethos, I'm doing it because I think this is the right thing to do.

I think you need: A) to believe in yourself, and B) resilience because it is not an easy or quick process. Personally, I had no choice because we wouldn't be able to eat if I gave up, but resilience is very important. I think it's also essential to have fun. I have a wonderful group of friends. I built my company, not for my children; I did it for me. Children don't give a toss what you are doing, as long as you are with them.

I've been a single parent for a really long time. It was very hard in the beginning because I had to wake up at 6am, get the kids ready, drop them off at school, come back, work, and then pick them up at 3pm. I've always worked from home: I just got bigger houses when my team got bigger. I would pick the kids up from school, be with them until 7pm. Then they'd go to bed and I'd start work again until midnight. Then I'd go to sleep and I'd start again the next day. I worked really hard and there was no balance to my life because it just wasn't possible. I admire people that achieve a work-life balance; I just didn't myself. That balance has come now: my social circle is more active and my life with my kids is more balanced.

To this day, I can't easily shop or buy clothing. My ex-partner would always take me into a shop and say, "Buy clothes." Most women would have loved this position, but I've never forgotten how it felt when I was homeless, I had little money, and I had £14 a day to feed four people. I'd go for long walks every night because I couldn't sleep and I'd walk around in Knightsbridge, because that is where my friend's house was, and I'd look in all the shops and I couldn't buy anything. Eventually, I stopped looking at the shop windows because it was the only way to manage. That's never gone away. I think that alpha-successful people are willing to take a high level of discomfort in pursuit of a goal.

In my background and my early beginnings, I was used to hardships, running on adrenaline most of the time and coping with the unexpected. What I had to do was 'learn to drop from survival into thrival.' I invented that phrase, but I believe in it. I wanted to find a way to learn how to thrive, not survive, because survival is ingrained. Culturally and gender-wise, I learned how to survive. That's not what I wanted for myself. So my internal work over the last year has been around: how do I have more fun? How do I actually thrive, not survive? How do I drop out of fear and flight, into rest and restore and rebuild? That's my goal now because I understand so much more of what it does to the body for people to live as I've lived. Stress kills. I'm not the only one doing this – there's nothing special about me. What's special about me is that I wanted a higher standard of living.

I'm really close to my kids. To me, that's one of the biggest achievements I've had in my life. People always talk about being successful and I consider my relationship with my children as a huge barometer of success. I think that you shouldn't give up the family for anything because that is not going keep you warm or happy. I have absolutely every intention of becoming a billionaire so I am not saying to give up on your goals. I'm just saying that you need to keep your eye on the ball with your family. I struggle when I see women going to work at 6am and coming back at 8pm and spending half an hour with the kids. I couldn't do that.

You have more choices than you think. And because I chose what I would not do, it enabled what I would do. So don't feel trapped. I hate that. Whenever I feel trapped, I'll blow up everything to change that feeling. So, eat well and work out – my body's the thing I take care of the most. My mind is the thing I take care of the second most. The kids are third and the business is fourth.

KATIE GODFREY

"We apply around 100 to 600 lashes on each eye. It's very, very different to doing it at home."

Job Title: Director/Founder of KG Salon and KG Professional.

Personal Bio: Creator of internationally-recognised KG Professional Eyelash Products. Multi award-winning business mentor and educator. A former model and founder of KG Modelling Agency, since opening her first beauty salon in 2009, Katie has launched training academies, a range of products, and franchising.

Business: KG Salon and KG Professional

Services:

KG Professional: Accredited eyelash training academy and professional product range for eyelash technicians. Business workshops and one-to-one mentoring.

KG Salon: Multi award-winning beauty salon. Treatments including nails, eye and brow treatments, waxing, lashes, tanning, HD brows. Franchised beauty salon brand.

Awards:

* Winner, 'LUX Salon Of The Year', 2017
* Winner, 'Client Experience Award', 2017
* Winner, 'Client Experience Award', 2016
* Winner, 'Most Outstanding Salon Of The Year', 2016
* Finalist, 'Eyelash Technician Of The Year', 2016
* Finalist, 'Training Centre Of The Year', 2016
* Winner, 'LUX Salon Of The Year', 2015
* Winner, 'Fans Choice Awards', 2015
* Winner, 'Eyelash Technician Of The Year', 2014

Contact:

T: 01582 883611

E: info@kgsalon.com

Website: www.kgsalons.com and www.kgprofessional.com

♦ ♦ ♦

My childhood was a bit mixed – growing up was great because we were always a close family. My mum and dad are like my best friends; they still are now. But I was badly bullied in school so that was really damaging. I left school at 13 with no qualifications at all. Obviously, this was a huge thing that affected me later in life. Because I left school so young, I didn't really have a clear idea of what I wanted to do when I was older. But I found modelling and I started doing that.

I was just shopping on Oxford Street with my mum. Someone came along and asked if wanted to be in a photoshoot and I said, "Yeah, why not." I gave it a go and that's how I got started. I found that when I was in front of the camera all my confidence came back; I got to be me as I didn't have anyone in the room judging me. I didn't wake up one morning and think, "Oh, I want to be a model today." I just got put in that situation and loved it. So everything happens for a reason.

I built my portfolio and over time I went to castings. It helped me get my confidence back and taught me a lot about how to build a business. I had to go to auditions and try to get a job, which is about trying to make a sale in that I was my business and I was selling myself!

There was a lot of PR and promotional work, fashion modelling, and a lot of swimwear modelling. I was really young, so there were limits to what I could do, but it was my full-time job - to the point that I moved to London at 17, on my own. It made it easier to attend castings. So, I've always been working, since I was 13. It's pretty crazy when you think about it.

My parents were a big help when I started; they used to take days off to take me to certain places if I needed chaperones because I was so young. I hated going anywhere local, because that's where the bullying was happening, so I'd be stuck in the house a lot of the time. Modelling kind of gave me confidence – it helped me to meet loads of people across the world, it taught me how to network online because a lot of it was Internet-based, trying to find photographers, jobs, and so on. That helped me to learn things that I still use today, so it was definitely in my favour.

One day I'd be in London, the next day Manchester, and then I'd be in Birmingham. I've done modelling in Europe as well; a bikini shoot and similar things. So I did get to do some travelling, but I stopped when I attempted the next part of my business, which was to open my own modelling agency.

I had about 250 models on my books. I was sourcing models and constantly searching for jobs and trying to persuade clients to come to our agency. It came naturally to me; I found it really easy because it was all I had known from the age of 13. I knew how to do it with my eyes shut so I felt like I needed another goal to stimulate me, so I could grow. Modelling was my safety net and it was what I always knew I could fall back on, but it was not something I wanted to do forever. It was my stepping stone to doing what I'm doing now.

What led you to move from modelling into setting up your own beauty salon?

Well, it was all rolled into one. I decided to open the modelling agency because I was getting loads of other agencies asking if I knew girls for this job or that job. And I thought, "Well, I'm going to start a model agency myself then and have girls working for me." That's why I opened the agency, but I was doing it from home in my parents' office so being in the house all day, every day, was a bit mind-numbing. My vision was that I wanted the models to come to me – I wanted to be able to measure them, I wanted to be able to do their portfolios and that type of thing. I couldn't do that based in an office at home.

So, I decided to get a building for it. But I was only a teenager and even though the business was doing well, it wasn't anything that would be able to cover rent and bills and provide an income as well. I had always said when I was younger, "I'd love a tanning shop," because being in modelling you always get treatments and you're doing that kind of thing all the time. There was a building I had had my eye on for a long time and I thought, "It's a really big building so I'm going to have half of it as a model agency, with a graphic studio, and the other half of it will be the tanning shop that I've always dreamt of."

I thought, "I'll figure out how to pay the bills." I told my mum and dad and they were like, "Oh my God, what is she doing?" I remember seeing the estate agent – at the time I was 19 – and I don't think they took me seriously at all. But I said, "Please, just trust me: I need this building." They let me have it, and that's when KG Salon started.

After just a few months, everyone locally was asking for all these other beauty treatments and I only did nails and tanning. I didn't really want to be a beautician and do beauty treatments, but there was such a big call for it. I thought, "I'm turning business away. It's clearly what the location needs." That's when I decided to shut down the model agency and turn the whole building into a salon. Then I had two large treatment rooms, a pedicure area, four nail stations, and an HD area. HD is a treatment specifically for waxing, tinting, threading, and reshaping of the eyebrows. It's a regrowth programme and clients come back every four weeks for it.

How did you fund your early business growth?

Half of it was from NatWest. I don't know how, to this day, I managed to get that money. Somehow, I managed to get a loan from them and the rest of the money my parents took out of their mortgage. I needed to buy the sunbeds, I needed to deck out the building, I needed treatment rooms, I needed stock, so I was up to my ears in debt. I thought, "That's it. I'm giving myself five years to clear this and after that I'm not having any more debt." Then I just worked my arse off for the five years to make sure I was out of debt and I paid my parents back 100% and I paid the bank loan 100%.

What was it like in the early days of your salon? What were the main challenges?

Exhaustion! I was shattered in the beginning because I didn't have staff; I only got staff six months in. I would work every day but Sunday. Every day I'd get up at the crack of dawn, I'd be working in the salon until 7pm, and then I'd go home and I'd still carry on working – because it was a new business and it takes a lot of work, time, and effort to build up a client base. Even though there was a call for salon services, I wasn't always fully booked because that takes time. So, I was marketing and advertising constantly, trying to figure out new ways to get more business and finding out what we needed to do to attract clients. The hardest thing was getting enough people in to be able to pay back all the money I'd been borrowing. I owed about £60,000 or £70,000. So the money was what kept me going because I didn't want to go bankrupt at such a young age.

It was so hard. After I hired staff, they were getting paid and I wasn't. What I always remember is I used to come home every Friday night and my dad would give me £40. That was all I had to get my lunch for that week and things like that. I used to pay my staff every week, but I couldn't afford to pay myself because I had to pay back everything else. Looking back, I don't know how I did it!

In the salon industry, business dips around October/November time because people are waiting until their Christmas treatments. I used to call my mum, crying my eyes out, saying, "I can't do it any more. I'd rather go under. I can't deal with this stress." She would help me get back on my feet by saying, "No, figure out why you've done this, why you've come this far." Because I didn't have any qualifications, I felt like I didn't have any other options. I didn't want to work behind a counter, I didn't want a normal job – I always wanted my own business and to be able to work for myself. So, my back was against the wall and I really had no option but for it to work.

How did it feel to be taking on staff when you had all these debts?

I started with Chloe, who still works with me to this day. She just worked 10 hours or so a week to begin with and we built it up over time. That gave me a little bit of a break as well, so that I could concentrate on other things like marketing and the business side. When clients started asking for treatments that I wasn't qualified in, I had to have staff who could do it properly and over time that just grew. The first three years were definitely the hardest, especially the quieter moments. Then it started getting easier. When it hit five years and I paid off all my debt, it was like a massive weight off my shoulders.

Your salon's won a lot of awards – how did these come about?

My first award was for Eyelash Technician of the Year in 2014. I had worked so, so hard. Every course I could possibly go on, I went on. I would study constantly, and discovered I had a massive passion for eyelash extensions. We went to the awards ceremony and I remember crying my eyes out when they called my name because I couldn't believe that I'd won this award. I'd thought, "Not in a million years will I win this!"

We've won quite a few awards since then. We won Fans' Choice Awards and LUX Salon of the Year, in 2015. In 2016, my training centre, which is my other business, was a finalist for Training Centre of the Year. We won Eyelash Technician of the Year again, Most Outstanding Salon of the Year, and the Client Experience Award in the same year. In 2017, one of my staff members was a finalist for Eyelash Technician of the Year; we won the Client Experience Award and we won LUX Salon of the Year Award, so we've won quite a lot of awards and have been really blessed in that sense. When I won Eyelash Technician of the Year, I was doing treatments all the time. Now that I don't do treatments, it's my staff who go up for the awards, so it still carries on our reputation.

What have been the defining moments throughout your journey – both the good and bad?

Well, the bad moments were the times when I was calling my mum saying, "I can't do it any more." Being bullied by other girls at school undermined my confidence so the thought of hiring staff who were *girls* scared the life out of me. But the only way to grow the business and be where I wanted to be was to have staff. As the business grew, I needed more staff. So, for things like being the boss, learning to be the boss, having standards to follow, holding team meetings and one-on-one sessions, I had to get over that fear. That was quite a big thing for me.

There have been loads of turning points. Deciding to shut the model agency and open a full-blown salon was the one thing that got us here. If I'd carried on with the model agency and hadn't listened to what the public wanted, my business might not have lasted. But responding to what clients wanted and running with that was a huge part of our success.

Also, opening my own product range was one of the big things. I used to buy eyelash stock from various suppliers because I couldn't find a company I loved that offered everything under one roof. So I decided to trial products, which took me about two years. I'd get products from here, there, and everywhere and trial them to see which ones I was happy with, which ones I thought would be the best on the market. That's how I started KG Professional, our own product range.

Now, I feel that we've got a product range for eyelash technician professionals that allows them to buy everything they need from one company, rather than having to go to different suppliers as I used to do. That business has been really successful.

What do you do today – what are the main areas of your business?

Day to day, I manage the staff, I teach, and I do business mentoring, as well as marketing for my business. The salon seems to run on its own now – my team of staff are fully booked constantly after nearly nine years in existence. We've got clients who come in every two weeks; it's just a really successful salon.

Then we've got the training side of the business. In the early days, when I was going to these training courses, there were times when I thought, "I would have done this differently or that differently." That's when I decided to start teaching and I discovered this love for training others; I absolutely adore it. So now we have KG Professional (that's our training academy) and we specialise in eyelash extensions. We have salons that come to us; we have therapists that come to us; we go to colleges and teach. For example, one of my trainers has five students that she was teaching today in eyelash extensions and those students would have come from all over the country. KG Professional goes hand in hand with our eyelash products: when we teach students, they use our products.

What is the KG product range?

The product range is for eyelash professionals. We've got glues, hundreds of different types of eyelashes for them to use, removers, eye-patches, everything that you would need to deliver a treatment to a high standard. People order online and we've got the distribution side that goes with that as well.

How do you differ from other salons offering similar treatments?

Sadly, it's hard to find a salon that purely does beauty, without dipping into other areas, like hairdressing. For example, you see a lot of hair salons that also do beauty and you have lots of different businesses under one roof whereas all my staff are employed by me and trained in beauty treatments. I'm not just renting out a chair or a space in my salon to others. It's just my brand and my girls that are employed. They work the way I want them to work and they work to a high standard. Our customer service is amazing. I think that makes a big difference to the quality of the customers' experience.

We have reward cards for our clients, so they gain points, and when they have enough points they get a free treatment. I think we're very, very different to any other beauty salon, which is why we're starting to franchise because I feel that this business model can be successfully replicated.

How did you go about building your brand?

I love branding, I'm very big into it. I've been able to take a step back now because people just see it as 'KG', rather than 'Katie Godfrey', but in the beginning, everyone saw it as me and used to relate it to me. So, clients always used to come to me and everything was always aimed at me constantly and that was quite hard. As we've grown and taken on more staff and expanded into social media, we've developed ways for people to contact the salon rather than just through me. With the reward system and our online presence – we have e-mail blasts – everything in our salon is branded to KG. We've got the product range which is KG so it's turned into this brand that people know and trust.

Clients used to contact me directly on Facebook or my mobile, but now they can book treatments online. They can book through our Facebook page, where someone else will get back to them rather than me, so people are not seeing me as the brand any more. Initially, it was quite hard because it was my baby, so I felt like, "No, I want everyone to contact me." But that wasn't possible when the salon started growing so big. You can't have everyone contacting you, so it was important to turn it into a brand that wasn't just me.

It's essential to get your logos right and make sure everything is the same across the board – your pricelist is the same as your appointment cards and your appointment cards are the same as your loyalty cards – and online you've got a certain way to talk to your audience. Finding out who your audience is and marketing to them: that's how I turned it into the KG brand.

We have over 4,000 clients in our flagship salon. We get between 20 and 30 new customers a week and we treat around 250 clients a week.

Are you planning to expand the main salon or are you happy to stay at the size and scale you're at?

It's something I've toyed with: "Oh, I'd love the salon to be this big or that big." But sometimes you can grow an individual business so big that you've got to think about how many extra clients you'd need to bring in just to cover the overheads. So instead of expanding our premises, I decided to expand as a franchise. This means that the salon I'm in now will stay as it is. It's a lovely salon, gorgeous, it's my baby. It's the thing that lifted me to where I am now. I'd like it to stay as the flagship salon and then franchise out and grow that way.

Otherwise I'd be scaling up all the time and thinking, "Oh my God, maybe we should move here, maybe I should move there." I have to rein myself in because sometimes you can just grow too big, too quickly. And actually we're doing amazingly already, so why change anything? I would rather create extra salons than make the salon I've already got any bigger.

How did you go about setting up and developing your training academy?

I started the training in 2012. We used to do training at the salon on Mondays because that was when the salon was closed. About four years ago, I went to New York to learn to do a certain method of eyelash. Everyone thought, "Why is she flying to New York? That's crazy." But I am a little bit like that – I just get an idea and I go for it. Even though it was expensive, and I flew to New York to do a training course that I could have done in London, I wanted to train with the person who I thought was the best in the world at the time. She had brought out this technique, which is called Russian Volume Lashes, and no one had really done them in the UK at that time. This was the moment when my teaching suddenly went crazy because everyone wanted to learn from me, because I'd been to New York and learnt this technique that people didn't know in this country. I had students all the time, coming from Ireland, from Scotland, from all over the country, to train with me.

That went from strength to strength, but right after I had my daughter, I stopped training because it wasn't top of my list. When she was a bit bigger, I decided to get back to it again. I have trainers – I have someone in Gloucestershire that works for us who has got her own salon, but she does KG training courses there. We're in the middle of moving to a new base in April, which is bigger, so we can train more students under one roof. We also go to colleges where we might teach eyelash training to 60 students at a time because they don't do that within their normal curriculum. Training is a massive part of the business; it's huge and growing and could bring a lot of opportunities in the future.

It also helps us in getting the brand out there. So it's not just the salon, it's not just the training, it's not just the products, it's not just the franchising. All the parts fit together to form the whole: the KG brand. If we go to a college and teach, that's 60 more students who know about our products, who know about our training, who know about our franchises. That's 60 more people who perhaps didn't know that much about us before they came on the course and now they know everything about us.

We have a beginners' course in eyelash extensions and a more advanced course. Then we do things like conversion courses. We do teach nails, too, though we haven't got branded products to go with that. The eyelash courses are the main part of the business.

In addition to the training, I also offer one-to-one business coaching for people within my industry because they want to know how I've done things, and I just love it. That's quite new; I've only been doing that about six months.

Would you say more people are wearing eyelash extensions nowadays? It used to be something that only movie stars did.

Yes, it used to be a very, very expensive treatment to have back in the day. When I started doing eyelashes, which was eight years ago now, we used to charge £95 for a basic set. It used to be a lot of money and not everyone could afford it. But it's become cheaper over the years and we now charge £55 because so many more people are doing it and the products have gone down in price. So, we can charge less for it, but then we've got more clients having it. That's for a basic set of lashes. For volume lashes, which are our most popular range, we charge £85 per set. They weren't so popular in the past because they were so expensive. Now, eyelash extensions are almost as popular as nails and people getting their nails done is like the bread and butter of the beauty industry. Eyelashes have taken off massively. Once the client starts having their lashes done, they're unlikely to stop and they'll be back every two weeks.

So they'll pay for their initial set and then they'll be back every two weeks at £35 to have them re-applied so they look brand new again. They'll come back to us with gaps in the lashes and then we fill in the gaps so they look like new. It takes about 30 to 45 minutes so if you've got a few girls doing that, it's a big business.

What is the difference between coming to your salon and doing your lashes yourself at home?

It's very different. At home, you can stick on cluster lashes and they might last for a weekend. Over time, they'll cause damage if they're not applied properly.

The lashes that we apply are individual lashes. One false lash is applied on one natural lash, so we'll be applying around 100 to 600 lashes on each eye. It's very, very different to doing it at home.

How do you combine being a mother with running a successful business? What are your tips?

I am a single mum and I have been since I was pregnant. Before my daughter came along, I was working in my salon every day as a full-time therapist as well as trying to run my business. I'd be working in the day on my clients and at night I'd go home and work on the business. Which, as everyone who's in business knows, is not the best way to do things. You need to work *on* your business rather than *in* your business and it was just something I had kind of got stuck in.

When I found out I was pregnant, I was thinking, "Oh my God. How am I going to do this, because I need to work every day?" Obviously, when you've got a baby you can't do that. I was the only person who did eyelashes at the time so I trained my staff exactly how I wanted them done, and how they should look, and how they should last, then my clients could switch over to them and be happy. I was so scared because I thought, "If these clients don't come back, it's going to have a massive impact on the business."

I had nine months to prepare so I talked to all my clients and I trained my staff in that period to the point where I was happy. My clients all went over to a new therapist and they were all happy and we managed to keep every one of them. So, my little girl has changed my life and the way I run my business.

You're constantly working when you have a business, anyway, so when she's sleeping I'm doing emails and I'm working from home more. I've managed to work *on* the business rather than *in* the business. I've still had that special time with my baby that I wouldn't have been able to have if I had to go into the salon every day. So, it forced me to change the way I ran my business, which actually (funnily enough) grew my business massively because I wasn't working on clients every day.

So even though it was so scary and daunting when I first fell pregnant, it changed the whole of my business in a positive way. And yes, it is hard to be a mum and manage a business; your phone is constantly going and you're under pressure and you're still trying to be a good parent at the same time. But she's always been brought up like that so now she'll even come to business meetings with me and sit quite nicely in the corner. She'll come to the salon and know how she should act in the salon. She's got a desk because she wants to work like mummy. She's been brought up that way. I feel that I still get to do my business, and grow it every single day, but at the same time still get to be an awesome mum and be with her and she only has to go to nursery twice a week.

You've never had a business mentor yourself. How did you work out how to build the KG brand and business?

It was mainly through trial and error. I read and read and read – things like autobiographies and business books. I read constantly and kind of figure it out that way.

I read Duncan Bannatyne's story, for example, and I read industry books. I'm reading one at the moment called *Business Nightmares* by Rachel Elnaugh off Dragons' Den. I read classics like *Think and Grow Rich* by Napoleon Hill. I read self-help books and management books by people like Tony Robbins and Michael E. Gerber. If I feel a bit down, I might motivate myself by reading. I will read to give myself time out from business and even though it's still work-related, it helps me to chill out.

What advice do you have for other women wanting to achieve what you have?

Don't give up is my main advice. Keep focused at all times. Positivity, I live by: what you put out there, you get back. Surround yourself with like-minded people. But mainly just keep focused and don't give up even if it gets really hard – and I don't think it ever stops being hard so just stay positive.

Did any of the girls who were bullying you at school ever come into your salon wanting to have their lashes done?

Yes, I've had them call me or their names have been in the diary, and I've thought, "Hmm, I really recognise that name." One of the main ones wanted me to train her in lashes. I don't hold grudges, but I sent her a really long email explaining why I didn't want to teach her and my reasons. She wrote back to me saying that she'd cried reading my email because she had no idea it was that bad. We were all young back then and we've all grown up and got families. This is what kids do, I guess, but it still has a massive effect on your adult life even though we were all kids at the time. I forgive them all now – it is what it is – but you never forget.

At the same time, I'm kind of grateful that it happened because I wouldn't be doing what I do now if I hadn't been bullied. I might never have had a beauty salon. I would probably have been a vet or something else, but I definitely wouldn't be here now if I hadn't gone through those troubles. If I had qualifications, I wouldn't have needed to fight as hard. So there's a positive from it.

TANYA MANN RENNICK

"My daughter had had a terrible car accident. I had to build the business while I was in the hospital with her – sleeping by her bed on a mattress on the floor, for about a month."

Job Title: Secret CEO Coach / Founder of the Oyster Club / Author of The Starr Principle

Personal Bio: I'm a mindset mentor and transform CEOs, partner level professionals and high achieving entrepreneurs to overcome stress, anxiety, adversity or challenging situations. Because I'm considered an authority on Mindset and Emotional Resilience, I've been invited to speak at the House of Lords and the European Parliament. As a professional speaker, I present motivational talks at many conferences, seminars and workshops in the UK and Europe.

Business: Tanya Rennick / The Oyster Club

Services: Turning Dissatisfaction into Fulfilled Leadership. Business Motivational Talk. Life Inspirational Talk. VIP 1-to1 Speaker Training. Corporate Presentation Skills Training.

Contact:

E: info@tanyamannrennick.com

T: +44 (0)1326340848

Website: www.tanyarennick.com

♦ ♦ ♦

I started my education at an all-girls school, which was very sweet. It was very old-fashioned and we did "eurhythmics", which was a sort of dancing with tambourines. Then the headmistress changed and no one liked the new one, so there was a mass exodus from the school. Not long after that, I started at a theatre school in

London called Sylvia Young Theatre School. It's famous now, but back then, it was just lots of fun. Half the week was educational and half was vocational and I think that was where I discovered my love of people. Because everything that you do in the world of acting is about understanding characters; that's really where I discovered my fascination with the dynamics of relationships. Ironically, it's also where I found that I really got bad stage fright!

What were your first jobs?

I had a foray into acting and the fear was just too painful. I spent about a year doing various acting jobs and it was very stressful. At the time, nobody had explained to me that it was very healthy to have fear, and you could turn that adrenaline into positive energy. So, I gave up the world of drama. I started to work, after that, in lots of different jobs. I went to work for my mum in her butcher's shop, briefly. Then I got into PR and I went to work in the city, which I really enjoyed. I thought that I had found my thing, but then there was a massive recession and I was made redundant. That knocked me back again with my self-esteem. I went back to work for my mother and that felt like I was taking a step backwards. Eventually I started to work part-time because I wanted to get a higher education. I did a foundation for my humanities degree and I fell in love with humanities, which spans a combination of history, philosophy, English, art, and I really loved it.

Then I eventually went into property search; acting on behalf of the purchaser/renter to save them time and money.

I did that for a while and that gave me a lot of pleasure because I love nosing around people's houses. I did mainly rentals and I enjoyed it. I must have done it quite well because eventually I was asked to do a pilot for a TV show about property hunting... It was like a version of Love It or List It. We filmed a pilot, but they chose to use Kirsty Allsop, so I was back to just being a property searcher.

Then when I was doing the property searching, my marriage came to an end and I realised that I had to do something that would generate a reliable income that I could do around my children. It also needed to be something that I would enjoy. It was a bit of a time of reinvention and I had started networking in order to help my property search business. I found it a real struggle to network; I was so shy. I used to walk into networking and shake, so for some strange reason I decided that if I hosted an event, I wouldn't feel quite so nervous. I had this idea that, 'I will invite all these people to a venue and I will be so busy hosting that I won't have to do all the embarrassing walking around and networking bit'. I know it sounds illogical, but it was the only way that I could do it.

How did you come to set up The Oyster Club in London?

I found that I was good at getting people to come to my events. I would go to lots of different networking meetings and there would always be a handful of interesting people at each event, and I would pick out those people and then invite them to mine. The idea was that I would filter out all the most dynamic people. The meetings grew and grew. I started to host them on the last Friday of the month, so they became quite celebratory and they had a party-like atmosphere. The provided an opportunity to forget your troubles and come and meet like-minded people and let your hair down a bit while making business contacts. I really liked the social element of them and I always used to say that this was a business *and* social network because you did business with people you liked.

It grew and then I did my property search less and less because that work was quite stressful and I found the networking infinitely more appealing. We had the meetings at The Champagne Bar and they handed out oysters at six o'clock, so it just became known as The Oyster Club. Then I had all these analogies that networking is a bit a like a filtration process; you are always looking for the perfect pearl. You can cut open lots of oysters until you find that pearl, and I guess that's a bit like networking in a way. Everything seemed to flow from that: I was the Mother of Pearl and I tweeted “Pearls of Wisdom.” The Oyster Club was like the umbrella meeting on the last Friday of the month: it was irreverent and there was no sort of meeting agenda. It was more a case of, "Come and have a drink from four or five in the afternoon." It would finish at around seven and that would be that. At its high point, with the drinks events, we had over 150 people and people still get in touch to ask me if I’ll consider hosting another one.

From there I created three membership clubs, two of which were successful and one that didn't quite take off. The first one was the Seed Pearl Club, which was a monthly breakfast meeting with about 30 people. It was all about growth, development, and learning. I would have someone deliver a workshop with a learning outcome. You would come and have the networking and the breakfast, and you would leave with a useful idea or technique that you could implement into your business—ideas from the practical to the pie-in-the-sky. We had everyone from compliance lawyers offering regulatory advice to Feng Shui experts telling you how to energise your desk. They were great!

Then, I had The Cultured Pearl Club, which was a monthly meeting in the evening and these were ideas around culture—philosophy, art, history. I had an art historian speaking about Salvador Dali, Pop Art, the Pre-Raphaelites, and perhaps most interestingly, the Femme Fatale in art and how she's depicted through the different ages. We had historians speaking about conspiracy of Jack the Ripper or what Georgian London was like, especially the history of the buildings. We had a philosophical debate discussing what telling lies and keeping secrets does to the soul. We even had a sexual psychotherapist posing the controversial question: is monogamy psychologically healthy? Nevertheless, even though all of these interesting events were I don't think I was as good at publicising this or attracting the right kind of audience.

Then we had The Black Pearl Club, which is still going strong to this day, ten years later. The Black Pearl Club is the ultimate because a black pearl is the most rare. The club is for allegiance in business: professionals at partner level, successful entrepreneurs, and decision makers. It's now a quarterly dinner, and it's generally black tie, always in a private dining room.

It's important that people are able to relax and network at quite a high level with fellow decision makers. Over the years, the format of this has changed, because I used to have speakers in all the time and now the format has slightly changed. I've had speakers like Jonathan Aitkin, Camila Batmanghelidjh (founder of Kids Company), John Bird (founder of the Big Issue), Barry Hearn the sporting events promoter, and Lord Jeffrey Archer. I've hosted quite fascinating and even sometimes quite maverick-type characters and that has definitely raised my profile. I now have opened it up so that I invite people to sponsor a dinner if they would like to and that's changed the dynamic slightly. Along the way it's helped me meet some interesting people and develop my coaching career, which was just a natural flow really.

Explain more about the ethos and feel of the club.

The ethos and the feel was trying to be the antithesis of what we've come to understand of typical business networking – I wanted it to be the opposite of the weekly breakfast with badges and false referrals and elevator pitches and the "Buy my widget" part of networking. It's about creating relationships based on personality rather than selling your service, because I think you want to assume that most people are good at what they do, so how do you then select who to work with? It boils down to personality and reputation. That's what you need to grow over time, so it's a slow-burning thing. It's all the personality that you bring to the table that singles you out as someone worth talking to.

We have a high level of people that attend. We have some investors, someone from a foreign exchange company, lawyers, high net financial advisors, business owners and so on. It's very exclusive, generally high net worth and you need to know the right people to get in. I don't think I could get into my club—let's put it that way! I think I'm the most under-qualified person in the room. The idea was make it elite without being stuffy so that you feel a sense of achievement because you're there. Generally, the way that you get in is because you know someone else who comes along or you contact someone and ask for an introduction. For example, if you wanted to come to a dinner, you would approach me, via LinkedIn or whatever, and say, "Do you think I'd be suitable for the dinner?" If someone calls me and asks me all the obvious questions like, "How many people?" I usually think, 'Well, they're out to sell,' so they're probably not going to be right for the dinner. Forty is the maximum we allow, but only if they're the right people. I think that's really important. It's supposed to be an indulgent, rewarding evening where you meet people with whom you share similar ideals, who are as driven or as aspirational as you are, or who have achieved already. So you're around those sorts of people. It's exciting.

These are not the kind of men and women you would bump into at your local supermarket, which is why I rely on the regulars to make introductions and bring new people in. It is an exhausting business and many people think they can easily start networking clubs. They think, 'Oh, let's just stick an advert on Eventbrite and Bob's your uncle.' It's not as easy as that. It is hard work. It does require you to constantly be out there, maintaining relationships and generating new ones and so on.

How does it feel to have founded such an exclusive club in London?

I'm very proud to see what I've created. I'm constantly critical and trying to improve it. I guess there are two schools of thought. You either think 'If it ain't broke, don't fix it' or else you think that there's always something you can do to intrigue. I'm constantly honing it and I'm learning on the job. I think that's the way that you keep it fresh. It's gone through lots of different looks and styles, but it's always maintained this air of exclusivity and elegance. Sometimes I've shot myself in the foot because it's not that easy to advertise and to publicise. It is about keeping this very fine balance.

You used to suffer from stage fright – yet you have spoken at the European Parliament and the House of Lords. How did that happen?

I was incredibly shy and I struggled to give an elevator pitch in front of a dozen people. I remember going to a networking event and we were all trying to improve and hone our sixty-second introduction. When it came to me, I was so nervous that I couldn't remember what I was even saying. My face was hot and my palms were sweaty; it was that bad. It culminated in attending a Christmas charity networking event and I won a raffle prize that I had to go and collect. Just crossing the room to pick up a bottle of wine—I felt like I was wading through treacle. It was pitiful. I took that bottle of wine home, opened it, and I drank it. I just sat there having a talk with myself and had the realisation that everything I wanted to achieve was being blocked by my fear; it was as if there was this barrier between me and everything I wanted to achieve. I had to get over the wall.

I read Susan Jeffers' *Feel the Fear and Do It Anyway*, which started the ball rolling on my personal development journey. It was as if the touch paper had been ignited and I consumed personal development with great enthusiasm from that point. I just went for it. I did a couple of courses locally. I started with Landmark, and then there was Essence; then I went to Anthony Robbins's event Unleash the Power Within. I became a firewalker. I went on to study with quite a few of the gurus and I read and read and read. I conquered my self-esteem issues. I healed myself and I realised that I was dealing with a different part of my ego. Once I sorted that out, there was no more fear. It was only a desire to impart information and what I had learnt and to share my knowledge. It really was a question of someone flicking on a light switch in my head. I realised how powerful our mindset truly is.

I gave a talk at an event I created called the Love Brigade, which was a pop-up charity event to help London's homeless during the month of February. The idea was that we were going to fill some bags – I called them bags of love – with useful items like food, toiletries, socks, gloves, hats, blankets, even a £5 gift card for Costa. I thought that maybe about 25 or 30 friends might get together and do this with me. I'd put a message out on Facebook and then this thing mushroomed. I didn't realise the power of my reach at that point. I knew that I had built a tribe around me, but I didn't really know my power at that point. From conception to reality was six weeks – and in those six weeks I had an amazing response. The BBC came to do an interview. I had 300 bags filled, with Love Brigade printed on them, and about 500 people eventually got involved. Someone came on board to do all the admin and co-ordination, since I'm a concept person and the logistics were becoming a nightmare. We had to get four areas of London to collect all these items and bring them together; we met in Westminster and we were able to get around 300 people to fill the bags, put them together, and take them out onto the streets. I was advised that I had to give a welcome to the people who had given up their time to come and help on a Sunday morning. Obviously, this is about leadership and making people feel that they've done a great thing by donating their time and their money and so on, so I gave a speech about togetherness and that went well. It had this incredible knock-on ripple effect: everyone who was there, then went out into their own local area and helped homeless people, looked at them like human beings, and gave them their time. It was a great, great thing. There was someone there at the event who saw me speak and asked me to come to the House of Lords and give a talk on mindset and female entrepreneurship and positivity.

It was thrilling and daunting at the same time.

How did you overcome your nerves?

I couldn't quite believe it. I stood outside the House of Lords having this surreal moment where I was thinking, 'I don't know if I deserve to be here. I'm not sure that this is right and what can I possibly tell people?' Then I had to give myself a talking to and say, "Well, actually you've got quite a lot to say on how you dust yourself down and bring yourself back up from the abyss." I knew that it was important, and even if I could help one person in that room I would have done a great job. I was so excited just passing through security and having my photo taken. Then you get a tag and I went through the House of Lords trying not to get my phone out to take pictures because you're not allowed. Then I went into the loo and I actually videoed myself saying, "I'm in the House of Lords. I'm so excited." I was just beside myself with excitement.

When I went in to give the talk, there were a couple of people before me and they were not terribly exciting with their delivery style, so the energy was quite low. So I thought, 'Okay. All I really have to do is just be me'. When you understand that, you can’t go wrong. You can be ill-prepared, you can mess up because of technical things, but you can't go wrong if you're you. I think that's my top learning experience from all of it. The talk went very, very well. These things have a wonderful domino effect. A few days after that, someone who had been present at the event called me and invited me to the European Parliament to give a talk. So, I did. It was very sort of Forrest Gump-y!

What was it like talking at the European Parliament?

I gave a similar talk, but not the exact same one because I've never given a talk off by heart. Once I had gone through that process, I did develop a signature keynote talk called The STARR Principle, which talks a little about my journey, the things I've learnt along the way, and how you need to shine from within and star in your story. I do now have a signature keynote, but then I was talking about mindset and the power of positivity. It was mainly speaking about women who are looking to get back into work following long periods of absence. You can be absent because you've had children, or you've been under-qualified so you've gone back to school, or you can be absent mentally because you haven't had strong enough self-esteem.

Tell me about your coaching.

As the relationships grew through my networking, I started hosting Master Mindset and helping people with their own decision-making process – because it became quite apparent that many people struggle around the area of decision-making. However successful they are, there is always this difficulty in making some of the hardest choices that we have to make, usually in our personal lives. You can be really successful at business, but you can really, really struggle around personal issues. I found that I was able to hone in and work out what was going on with someone almost instinctively. My clients are always quite astounded that I can understand what their issue is so quickly. I'm very lucky to be able to do the work that I do. I get a lot of pleasure from watching someone with anxiety issues, or whatever is causing their problems, to getting them through to the other side. It's massively rewarding. It's the culmination of all the work I've done with The Oyster Club, and I now have the courage and confidence to do this work and do it well. I'm really happy that I'm able to work as a coach.

What are your lightbulb moments over the years while setting up The Oyster Club?

With The Oyster Club, I knew very little about setting up and running my own business. The lightbulb moment was that if I pulled together a team who knew all the stuff that I didn't, I could excel at the things that I did the best and grow my business. The second lightbulb moment happened when I realized that I was doing what I enjoyed and doing it really well. I know that phrase is a bit overused: do what you love and you'll never work another day. It's not quite true because work is work and you do have to apply yourself, but if you do something that you love you will put more energy into it and you will relish doing it and do it well.

With speaking, the best advice I can give is that the thing that will make you most nervous is lack of active preparation. If you know what you're going to say, and you believe what you say to be true and useful, then you won't be nervous. If you do not believe in what you're about to say, or you haven't prepared thoroughly enough, you will be. There's no two ways around it. That applies to well-seasoned speakers as much as novices. For me, speaking is a way to connect with people. So, if I feel like even one person gets what I'm saying, then it's worthwhile. Speaking has been wonderful experience and I thoroughly recommend it.

What are you proudest of?

When I think about some of the big moments in coaching, it just makes me want to cry. Life coaching is incredibly personal, and most people never want to admit to their vulnerabilities and never want to say that they've been to a coach. I work with seriously successful people, the kinds who aren't ever allowed to admit their weakness. They will message me and say, "Tanya, I can't thank you enough. I thought I was going mad." Things like that, but they won't share with anyone else.

It's so rewarding to know that I've helped someone get back on track who had sort of lost their mojo. Often it will be around the areas of life balance, troubled relationships in the workplace or at home. I receive these messages that I've had such a positive impact and it's just the most incredible feeling. It's very humbling.

I do a Mastermind group for people who can't work with me one-to-one. My group WhatsApp is always pinging is my phone. They write to me saying, "You've been our rock. Whatever we can do for you we will." And it's just, wow!

To be recognised for what you do and have people appreciate and want more of it is the most rewarding, life-affirming thing in the world. Nothing beats that feeling of being satisfied that I'm serving and have a purposeful life.

What advice do you have for others wanting to achieve what you've done?

The advice is: stop looking for reasons why not and look for reasons why you should. Women tend to be quite detail driven and are not willing to be experiential learners. They want to read a book about the specifics or get a qualification or train in something before they go and do it. They hate making mistakes and never want to appear like they don't know something. Men tend to be quite happy to learn as they go. It doesn't matter: unless you're going into brain surgery, you don't need to know everything before you begin. Life is a continual learning process, so I do not ever feel that I've learnt enough. Although other people might call me an expert, I'm still learning, so I'm constantly learning and improving and trying new ways of getting advice from people.

My advice would be to have the confidence to start and continue learning. Don't be afraid to ask for help; you can't do it all. As women, we're afraid to look like we're not coping and so we do too much. I'm as guilty of it as anyone. The sort of crazy, plate-spinning woman is not really the archetype we want to follow. At some point, this idea of was instilled that we should be the super-woman, super-capable, omnipotent being and it's just a fallacy. We can't be; we just can't be. So, learn to delegate, learn to say no, learn to not do everything yourself and not everything needs to be done. While writing her first book, J.K Rowling famously didn't clean her house for about three years. So let go of some of it. It doesn't all have to be done perfectly in order to achieve this super-woman status. Lots of really successful people have let certain things go. If you can afford to hire help then do, and if you can't afford to hire help, then just let it go. That's quite a big one. Also, I'm really, really hot on life balance and that's one of the areas I help people with because you can burn the candle at both ends and make yourself incredibly ill. You need this balance of work and rest and recreation time. Rest and recreation are two different things; you can't lump them all in one. Take yourself out for a lovely walk and perhaps have a nice lunch out somewhere. That's me time. It's about treating yourself, making time to have thinking time, creative time, reading time. You need to be able to factor in some alone time.

My other advice is: don't let people tell you that you can't do something. Lots of people told me I couldn't. You have to have a fairly thick skin. You have to be prepared that you will lose certain friends along the way. You want to know when you can switch off and you want to know when you can turn up the energy. I put in very long hours at the beginning. When I started The Oyster Club, it was very new, and my daughter had had a terrible car accident; her skull was fractured in two places and initially she was in a coma, so I had to build the business while I was in the hospital with her. I slept by her bed, on a mattress on the floor, for about a month while we were in hospital while trying to launch a business that was a few months old. It took a lot of gumption. I didn't realise it at the time. I just thought I had no choice; I'd started and I couldn't let it go. I had the bit between my teeth. At exactly the same time, I was also going through a divorce and I had two little boys to deal with as well. I was completely exhausted by that. I really, really was. I look back now and I think, 'Now that is some plate spinning.' That really was. Now that I'm able to look at it a bit more objectively, I do not know how on earth I did it. I just think that I was very gutsy.

Sometimes things will push you to your limit and then at other times, nothing much happens. You need to keep up that momentum when it happens. Momentum is a powerful thing. The Oyster Club is an old *Grande Dame* now and has an energy all its own. It's something I'm very proud of.

NOEL JANIS-NORTON

"I want every parent who yearns to have a calmer, easier, happier family life to be able to learn how."

Job Title: Director, 'Calmer, Easier, Happier Parenting and Teaching'

Personal Bio: Noel Janis-Norton is a learning and behaviour specialist, public speaker, and author of eight books on parenting and teaching, two of which have been Amazon UK bestsellers. She is the Director of 'Calmer, Easier, Happier Parenting', a consultancy and training organisation that works worldwide with families and schools, teaching skills for success at school and harmony in the home. Noel has created programmes and resources that enable her team of practitioners to successfully address a wide range of issues, from the typical concerns of most parents and teachers through to more extreme problems.

Business: Calmer, Easier, Happier Parenting and Teaching

Services: Parenting advice via books, CDs, courses, talks, private consultations; advice for teachers via books, teacher training, talks, school observations, and feedback.

Contact:

E: admin@calmerparenting.co.uk

Website: www.calmerparenting.co.uk

♦ ♦ ♦

Both my parents were intellectual and bohemian and left-wing. I grew up surrounded by ideas and ideals, art and literature and music, with a love of reading and language and words. My mother had dreams of being a published author herself, but ended up writing advertising copy and being a ghost writer for others. She always had it in the back of her mind that either I or my sister would become a writer, but sadly she didn't live to see that happen.

I moved around a lot in my childhood and adolescence, mostly in New York but also other countries – France, Italy, Israel, England, Scotland. I went to many different schools – some state, some independent, some traditional, some very progressive – and one result of this was that whatever school I attended I was always different from my classmates. Their clothes were different from mine, their slang was different, their accents were different, the music they listened to, the teachers' academic expectations – all of that was different, so I never felt that I fitted in.

I never felt comfortable. I was always desperate to be just like everyone else. It took me years to realise that that was a silly goal and now I'm happy to be either similar to or different from other people. It doesn't matter to me now, but it was a huge worry for me when I was a child and a teenager. I became very anxious, full of self-doubt – a perfectionist. I never felt that I was good enough and that feeling, unfortunately, has stayed with me.

What jobs did you do after you left school?

When I was a teenager, I did a lot of childminding to earn pocket money because money was tight at home. I found that I really enjoyed it and that I had a way with children. I also worked in an office one summer and I realised that wasn't the sort of job I wanted to do.

When I went to university, I decided to study literature because I loved reading. Then I realised that there was no career path for a graduate with a degree in literature, at least not in New York when I was growing up, so I decided to transfer to my second favourite subject, psychology. But at the age of 18, with all my insecurities, I just couldn't visualise myself having the confidence to be a psychologist and I didn't have anyone to reassure me and say, "Well, of course, without experience, why would you expect yourself to have the confidence to think you can do this?"

Having decided that I couldn't possibly be a psychologist, I didn't know what to study at university and it was really bothering me. One day at breakfast, my mother said, "Why don't you become a teacher?"

Since I had never thought of that in my life, I said with astonishment, "A *teacher*?!"

"Yes," my mother said. "You like children and you're good at explaining things."

"A *teacher*?!"

"Well, it can be your day job."

You see, everyone in my family was something special – either a musician or an artist or a writer – so the assumption was that I would also be something highly creative. But I still said, "A *teacher*?!"

Then my mother said, "You could travel." My family loved to travel so that would be a big plus.

"How could I teach in another country if I can't speak the language?" I asked.

"Do you remember the short story by Aldous Huxley, *Young Archimedes,*" she said, "where the older boy teaches the younger boy mathematics just using a stick, writing in the dirt?"

I had run out of objections so even though I wasn't enthusiastic about it at all, I transferred to the university's college of education. I was surprised to find that I really enjoyed learning about education.

By the time I graduated I knew a lot about teaching, in theory, but it very soon became obvious that I had been taught nothing useful about classroom management or behaviour control or motivating pupils. On my first day in the classroom I was so out of my depth that I thought, "Teaching is not for me. I've wasted four years of teacher-training college because I can't do this."

That very first day at lunch I asked the other teachers how they managed their classes. "How do you get them to sit down and listen and do what they're told?" I asked. One teacher told me that the children were animals so not to bother even trying to get them to behave! Another, a seasoned teacher, said, "Oh, don't worry, you'll get the hang of it in a few years." But I thought, "I won't last a few years."

I didn't get any useful advice on classroom control, even from the teachers who were very good; they had been doing their job for so long that it was second nature to them and they didn't even know how to put into words what they were doing that got such good results. They gave me vague advice, like "Have high expectations" and "Put your foot down." The trouble was that I didn't know how.

I realised that if I were going to survive as a teacher, I'd better learn quickly. So, at every opportunity, I focused on observing the teachers who were really good at bringing out the best in their pupils. I watched carefully and listened carefully to what those teachers said and how they said it, even paying attention to their body language. I made notes, then went home and studied my notes, and the next morning in class I would experiment.

I expected that within a few months, things would start to improve. I was amazed that in fact it took less than a week to see a big shift in the pupils' willingness and participation. That's when I realised that teaching is not an arcane art – it's a skill, and you can learn it.

Was there a defining moment that made you change everything?

A defining moment in my move towards becoming a parenting advisor came a few weeks later, when the parents noticed that I could manage their children and started asking me for advice about how to get their little tearaways to behave: "How can I get him to do his homework, or go to bed, or do what he's told?" I wasn't yet a parent at that point so I had no idea what to recommend. I just explained what I had been learning and practising in the classroom and suggested that maybe they could try those techniques at home.

Within a week, the parents came back to me, delighted that my tips were working. That's when I realised that teaching and parenting operate along the same principles. It was a lightbulb moment.

From that point on, I gave advice to parents at the school gates whenever they asked. Then I decided to put it all into writing so that I wouldn't have to keep repeating myself. It started out as a one-page list of tips, which soon grew to a booklet and then a series of booklets.

Eventually, I realised it was time to gather all my advice into a book, but I found that unexpectedly difficult. It was so frustrating because I couldn't work out how to get all my ideas in the right order; I felt like I needed to say everything first before I could say something else. So, I procrastinated about writing a book for years, occasionally feeling brave enough to tackle it, but mostly feeling overwhelmed. Instead, I concentrated on teacher-training, on leading parenting courses and workshops, and on private consultations with parents.

That might have been the end of my career as a writer, but luckily I was approached by a small publishing company that specialises in educational books, Barrington Stoke. They commissioned four books from me in just under three years: two books for teachers and two books for parents. Having a deadline did the trick! Writing still wasn't easy or comfortable, but I had to get the books written by the deadlines so I did.

Once I had written those four books, I felt I could rest on my laurels. I wasn't planning to write any more books, just booklets and tip sheets for my clients. I did write and produce a series of audio-CDs on a range of parenting topics, and they sold very well here and in the U.S.

Then, one day, everything changed. The actress Helena Bonham Carter, who was a client, mentioned in a newspaper article that I had helped her and her husband with some parenting issues. The day after the article appeared, a swarm of publishers and an agent contacted me out of the blue. And even though I had given up on the idea of writing another book, I thought that since these strangers had gone to the trouble of emailing me, it would be only polite to meet with them!

When I met the agent Clare Hulton, I was so impressed with her that I took her on. She said that I shouldn't limit myself to the publishers who had contacted me, but that she would approach some other publishers as well.

I had meetings with lots of publishers and I gave each of them some of my audio-CDs so that they could find out what 'Calmer, Easier, Happier Parenting' was all about.

Many of these publishers had children, so after they had listened to the CDs they naturally began experimenting with the parenting strategies that I recommend. When they saw for themselves that these strategies work, they were very keen to publish me.

I was so naive about the publishing world that I would have accepted the first offer, but my agent took charge and we ended up with a bidding war, which was so exciting. The very first offer was for £30,000 and the final offer, that I accepted, was for an advance of more than £200,000. I had never seen that much money before in my life and of course by the time I had paid hefty taxes on it, it was nowhere near that much.

The funny thing is that even though I no longer teach in a classroom, I'm still a teacher. I'm teaching parents and teachers, which is very fulfilling, and also lots of fun. Instead of teaching just being my day job, as my mother predicted, teaching is my passion.

How did you come to set up your parenting centre? That was quite a bold and brave thing to do.

I started the centre when I was living in the United States, in a small city, and it just happened organically because so many parents were asking for advice.

When my children left home to go to university, I left home also; I moved from the U.S. to the U.K., which had been my dream since I was a teenager. Once I was settled in London, I set up a centre again and it grew quickly and to a much bigger scale because London is so much bigger.

I became known through word of mouth. Parents and headteachers, even doctors and psychologists and social workers, recommended me. Over the years, I have had quite a few celebrity clients, but unfortunately I can't say who they are! Helena Bonham Carter was just about the only one who was brave enough to go public. For too many parents, there's still a stigma about asking for parenting advice or support.

It's seen as an admission of weakness, even of failure. But I believe that asking for help is a sign of strength and commitment to the well-being of one's family. Despite the myth, parenting doesn't come naturally to most of us, especially modern parenting, which is much more complex and stressful than it was for earlier generations.

What are the main areas of your work and business today?

We work with parents and teachers and with anyone else who works with parents or children. I give seminars and lectures, run courses, and do teacher-training (including going into schools to observe and then coach the teachers). I have consultations with parents all over the world via Skype. I do home visits.

I do something we call 'Family Learning Sessions', which includes both parents and one child. I teach the child something; it could be something academic or something to do with behaviour or it could even be a social skill. As I demonstrate the parenting and teaching strategies, the parents are watching, asking questions, learning how to do it so that they can replicate it when I'm not there.

When children or teens are having problems at school, I go into the school to observe and then I give recommendations so that the staff and the parents can work together to improve outcomes.

How many books have you written?

I've written eight books in total. The first four were with a very small publisher, as I mentioned. The next four were published by Hodder & Stoughton. This is the 'Calmer, Easier, Happier' series. The first and the third books in this series were Amazon U.K. bestsellers: *Calmer, Easier, Happier Parenting* and *Calmer, Easier, Happier Boys*.

How did you develop your brand of 'Calmer, Easier, Happier Parenting'?

Originally, there was no brand at all. As I developed my ideas over time, I knew that I wanted a title that would capture the whole method. I spent a fair bit of time pondering it, but nothing occurred to me. Then one day I was walking in the countryside and what popped into my head was: *calmer, simpler, happier*. I thought, "Oh, that's perfect. That's it." A few days later, I started worrying that it might sound as if I'm saying that the children are simple, as in 'simple-minded', so I thought I had better change it. So, I went back to pondering. Soon what came to me was *calmer, easier, happier*, and that became my brand for the books, for the CDs, for the name of the centre, and for the parenting and teaching methods I've developed.

Tell me about the defining moments in your business that have helped you to move forward.

It's not exactly a defining moment, but I've been propelled by the realisation that this method works for all kinds of parenting and teaching issues. And I want every parent who yearns to have a calmer, easier, happier family life to be able to learn how. My mission is to reach everyone on this planet who wants to learn how. This defines me and my work.

Do you think that came from your parents?

Yes, both my parents cared a lot about justice and equality and helping people, which is something that I absorbed as I was growing up.

What challenges did you face while you were setting up your business?

The challenges were, and still are, internal – my anxiety and perfectionism. Perfectionism isn't only about trying to do everything just right; perfectionism also results in a lot of procrastination. I think I can't do something well enough, which is so depressing that I put off even starting. Or else I do start and carry on for a while, but allow myself to get side-tracked when I get discouraged. I torment myself a lot.

Following through doesn't come easily to me, which gives me a lot of empathy for anxious and overwhelmed parents and teachers. I think that's part of why the methods I've developed are so successful: because I understand the need for support and hand-holding and step-by-step accountability when people are trying to change entrenched habits.

Were there any moments where you felt like giving up: like going back to your job or doing something completely different, for example?

I never felt like getting a job where I would be working for someone else because the few times I did that, for example when I was working in a school, my ideas were so different from those of the senior leadership that it made things very uncomfortable. I knew that I needed to be my own boss, to be an entrepreneur, even though I also knew that I don't have some of the qualities that everybody says you're supposed to have to be a successful entrepreneur: an unrelenting drive, confidence, self-motivation.

Give an example of where there was conflict between your take on children and the school's.

Most schools don't have a consistent policy on classroom discipline. Maybe they do on paper, but in practice they don't. Because I believe that consistency is very important, I came into conflict with the senior leadership. Interestingly, some staff members felt that I was too modern and 'touchy-feely', while others felt that I was too old-fashioned and 'strict'.

I'll give you an example. I was doing some consulting work in a secondary school that had a big problem, as many schools do nowadays, with pupils being on their mobile phones during lessons. The teachers hadn't earned the pupils' respect. The teachers didn't know how to take charge in a way that would teach the pupils to follow the rule of 'No mobiles in class'. So, the school made a rule that if a pupil took out a mobile phone in class, the teacher would immediately confiscate it and it would only be given back to the pupil's parents, who would have to come in to school to collect it. The hope was that this policy would discourage pupils from being on their phones during lessons and it was working as long as the school followed through consistently.

In one class that I was observing, I saw a boy take a mobile phone out of another boy's lunch bag, with that boy's permission. The teacher confiscated it, according to the policy. But the two boys pleaded with the teacher and said it wasn't fair and then their classmates joined in the argument. The teacher gave in and decided not to follow through with the consequence for the boy who owned the phone because he wasn't the one who took it out of his lunch bag. And that was inconsistent! If the mobile had been taken *without* the owner's permission I would have agreed, but he had said, "yes", so I felt that the policy should have been followed.

This might seem like a tiny, unimportant example, but little things like this happen in schools all day long and children and teens very quickly learn which of the staff are not going to follow through. And that leads to an erosion of respect and then to more ignoring of the school rules.

Do you think that teachers and heads don't have enough time or energy to follow through, given how many pupils they're dealing with?

Following through consistently actually *saves* time and takes much less energy so that's not the reason that teachers aren't consistent. It's because they haven't been taught effective skills and because they often don't have the support and backing of the senior leadership, who are themselves often overwhelmed and confused.

Unfortunately, a lot of teacher training is not very effective. Planning for professional development courses is often delegated to someone in the school who signs teachers up and the teachers may or may not get to choose what their training will be about. Teachers go off and do a one-day training and then they come back into the classroom and are overwhelmed again. Learning any skill requires more than just one day's exposure. It requires a trainer who will give useful feedback. This is why it's so much more effective when I do classroom observations, then coach the teachers, then observe them again some time later. That's how people learn.

What are your aha moments over the years?

An important aha moment, in a funny way, was when I admitted to myself that I enjoy almost everything about writing except the actual writing. I love thinking about the topic, planning what I want to say, organising my ideas in the most user-friendly order. I love making notes and adding to my notes. Then, after I've written it, I love proofreading and editing and expanding the material. But the actual process of turning my notes into sentences and paragraphs and chapters is what I find very difficult because I keep thinking it's not good enough.

Another aha moment was the realisation that a way around this problem is to get help, which is what I do now. Sometimes the help I need is just moral support and encouragement and empathy. Sometimes I get help thinking through something I feel stuck about. My sister helps me with this because she is also a 'Calmer, Easier, Happier Parenting' practitioner and because she has a very sharp, analytical mind. Sometimes I dictate the words to someone; that's easier for me because I love to talk. My sister and my friends are incredibly helpful. Writing is still not easy for me, but it's much easier than it used to be.

What do you feel is your biggest success or achievement?

Professionally, I'm very proud of my two bestsellers and I'm very proud that I've developed such a useful parenting and teaching programme, even though I didn't invent all of it myself. Some of it I developed myself, but other bits I gleaned from other sources and then I put it all together into a comprehensive package.

Every week I get emails and cards from parents and teachers telling me about their successes using the 'Calmer, Easier, Happier' methods and that feels terrific. I'm also proud that I've trained other practitioners, in a number of countries, and that their work with families and schools is very successful. In a small way, I do feel that I'm helping to make the world a better place, one family at a time and one classroom at a time, and I'm very proud of that.

How many people's lives do you think you've touched through your centres and books?

It's very difficult to quantify because I don't know how many people have read my books and listened to the CDs.

We're a not-for-profit organisation, and we're committed to never turning anyone away if they can't afford our fees, so we do one or two free events every month. Lots of parents come to those and then there are the private consultations as well. And we give talks for parents in schools and in the workplace, plus the teacher training.

I'm 73 and I've been doing this work since I was in my twenties. So, the 'Calmer, Easier, Happier' methods have probably reached tens of thousands of parents and teachers over the years and I'm very proud of that.

What would you say differentiates you from other parenting experts in terms of your methods?

In a lot of ways, my advice is similar to what parents would find in other parenting books and programmes. One of the big differences is our emphasis on consistency because consistency is so important in creating a calmer, easier, happier family life or classroom. All the experts tell parents to *try* to be consistent and then they mostly leave it at that because, given that modern life has so many variables, teaching someone how to be consistent requires lots of explanation and lots of examples. And that's what I provide. That's why my books are so big and why our talks and private consultations are so effective.

Our methodology also focuses on preparing for success to make it more likely that family life and school life will go more smoothly, rather than mostly focusing on what to do after things have gone wrong.

Another thing that every parenting book recommends is that parents be united in their decisions and in their follow-through because parents often unintentionally undermine each other. I agree, of course, but I recognise that this can be difficult to achieve so I don't just say it's a good idea – I teach parents how to become united. These are some of the ways in which this programme differs from others.

What advice would you give to others who want to achieve what you have?

If you've got anything that's stopping you, get help with it. Don't think you have to struggle on alone, which is what I thought for a long time. If you can't afford to pay for the help you need, get help from your friends and family. That's what I've done. You'd be surprised how pleased and honoured people feel to be asked to help.

What about balancing home and work life?

My children are in their fifties now, with partners and children of their own. I live alone so my home life now is exactly how I want it to be. But when my children were growing up, one of the ways that I balanced work and family life, and also doing things for myself, was by getting up very early and doing lots of work before the children even woke up.

What are your plans for the future?

I have ten more books lined up in my brain, just waiting to be written. There is so much about parenting and teaching that I want to say. I want to write and publish at least one book each year for the next ten years. That will keep me occupied and out of trouble until I'm 83.

In addition to the writing, which as I've said doesn't come easily to me, I plan to keep doing a lot of things that do come easily to me, the things that I love to do. I love working with clients, I love doing the teacher trainings, I love giving the talks and the courses and the seminars, so I'll continue to do all of those. I love doing these things in other countries as well, since I enjoy travelling very much.

The teacher training is very, very important to me. Each teacher influences so many pupils so when I can help teachers to be more successful, I'm reaching more families and more children.

Is any one of those ten unwritten books in your mind particularly important to you?

Many years ago, when my own children were little, I developed a method that teaches children to read (both decoding and comprehension) very easily and quickly. That's one of the projects I would love to expand. This reading method is called 'Abracadabra', and it's just as effective with struggling older readers as it is with children who are just starting school.

I'd like to publish this programme and I'd like to see it being used in every primary school because for children it takes the angst out of learning to read and for teachers it takes the angst out of teaching children to read. It's so easy and so quick – and it's fun.

This method of teaching reading is not completely different from what schools do now, but there are a few important tweaks which make the process much easier and quicker to master. You can take five-year-olds coming into Reception in September, and by Christmas most of the class can be reading fluently and understanding just as well as pupils in Years 2 or 3 can.

GILL ORSMAN

"Flowers identified who I was: they put me on the map. I really was one of the first people to go out there and do that particular type of photography."

Job Title: Creative Director and Owner, The Holistic Photographer

Personal Bio: Gill gained international recognition through specialising in still life and fine art photography, which led to many varied commissions in the world of advertising, design, packaging, and publishing. She became a unique specialist in Flower Photography.

Her latest photography now encapsulates the 'Beauty of Light' – quite literally 'Seeing the Unseen.' She has been capturing orbs in her photographs since 2009 and is now raising the awareness for this virtually unknown phenomenon.

Business: GILL ORSMAN ~ The Holistic Photographer

Services: I am a creative visionary and intuitive problem solver. People come to me for consultation, guided visualisation, mentoring, and spiritual guidance because I work within the realm of the Unseen. 'Seeing the Unseen' for me encapsulates wellbeing, healing, and higher consciousness photography. It is my belief that everybody is capable of creating an extraordinary life for themselves.

Contact:

E: seen@gillorsman.com

Website: www.gillorsman.com

♦ ♦ ♦

I had a happy childhood: I spent a lot of time outdoors whenever I could, in the forest and fields, exploring and climbing trees. I was given a Kodak 110 instamatic camera when I was eight years old and that sealed my destiny. The irony, funnily enough, is that when you used that camera, you needed to be at least three feet away from a subject to have it sharp. I remember that, because I was so inquisitive, I would get right up close to things and photograph them and they came out completely blurred. Little did I know. Years later, I made my name using that technique: a very blurry, soft-focus sort of feel, and it was almost as if it began back then because I just loved the whole medium of film.

I wasn't great at school. I really struggled with learning and reading although I loved music, art, and games. I excelled in art because I was always creative, always making things, so it was obvious that I should go on to art college.

I left school at 16: I finished with next-to-no exam results other than Art and Metalwork 'O' Levels. I failed all my other exams. Many years later, in fact only recently, I found out I am dyslexic and that's explained why I've had such trouble reading and learning over the years.

I went to art college because I wasn't really interested in anything else. We did a foundation year where I got to do many different subjects on creativity. Then I realised that this particular college didn't have much to do with photography at all so I managed to get a place at Epsom School of Art and Design. Here, I trained in all aspects of photography – somewhat a solo journey, as I was the only person specialising in photography that term. All my other friends were doing fine art, graphics or illustration so I was always downstairs on my own in the photographic studio with the tutors. Actually, that's been a regular occurrence throughout my life: I was quite a loner as a child, but happy in my own company, discovering things.

I got a lot of attention because no one else was studying photography and towards the end of the year we started working towards our diploma shows. I didn't really have any sense of what I was going to be doing when I left; I hadn't thought that far ahead. We had our end-of-year shows and this chap who was an ex-student came back to see them. He just happened to be working in London with a big-name photographer at the time. We got talking, because I was the only person with a photographic stand, and he said, "I'll see if I can get you some work experience with the guy I'm working with." I thought, "Really? Wow. Okay. Thanks!" So, we swapped numbers and he did exactly that: I had my first opportunity to work with Tony Heathcote at his studio in Kensington. It was so exciting and I learnt so much.

I remember us working on Pipers Whiskey in about 1980. I was fascinated because Tony was a still life photographer and he was doing an advertising campaign trying to promote this product. Then he had another shoot, on location, for a big mail order catalogue which was very well-known and successful in those days. He had to shoot a whole range of products and he had his own holiday home in Wiltshire. We went down to this fantastic cottage, with its own grounds, and did the outdoor shoots. We had a table laid out with all the products. At the end of the shoot, Tony had a wrap party, got quite drunk, and offered me a job for when I left college. I got on really well with everybody and now I was part of the team and that was it. So, I didn't even bother to look for a job. I was very lucky – I was in the right place at the right time.

I left college and went straight into my first job with Tony and I didn't realise how brilliant that was until I got so many phone calls from other students asking for jobs as assistants. "Nope," I'd say. "I've got it. Sorry. Goodbye." I became a second assistant and we had a fantastic time; I loved it. We were working with some big clients and on some big projects; I really enjoyed the whole process. But I think Tony had overstepped the mark thinking he could hire two assistants. Work is up and down anyway when you're self-employed, so I think that at a certain point he felt he needed to go back to one assistant, so he had to let me go.

I worked with Tony for about six months and then went on to work for other photographers in London, including Adrian Mott and David Fairman in Smithfield Market EC1, then finished my assisting apprenticeship with still life photographer Martin McGlone, back in Kensington. That building was full of 'big name' photographers, so I was right in the heart of creative energy. I made my transition to working as a full-time photographer based at those studios at 59 South Edwardes Square and I went on to became a commercial still life photographer based in London.

What made you decide on flowers as your specialism?

During my early years as a photographer, I went through a spell of stress-related illness and was off work for six months. I remember being quite depressed and struggling to find my niche in a very competitive and male-dominated field. When I came back, I struggled because I was a jobbing photographer. I was starting to get more work, but in our industry, you need to specialise in a particular niche in order to make your name. I wasn't really drawn to anything: fashion or car photography or food photography or portrait photography, just still life.

One day, a friend invited me to a private view exhibition at the AOP Gallery in London called Bloomin' Marvellous. It was sponsored by a florist who was unknown at the time, Paula Pryke and it was wonderful. I remember feeling really uplifted and I thought, "Oh, what a fantastic idea." The exhibition featured many photographers who had shot the odd flower in their time and I remember it was a delightful experience to be surrounded by such beauty and colour.

I was driving to work the next day and it hit me: "Wow! Flowers. I would love to specialise in that." I realised nobody was really doing it. After I had parked the car and walked to the studio, I opened the main front door and there in the centre of the hallway was the head of a beautiful flower – a gerbera. I knew instantly this was for me. It was like a sign from the universe that I was on the right path. I picked it up, put it on my desk, and that was the beginning of the new phase of my career, becoming a specialist in flower photography.

I got together with a friend, an art director at Marshall Cavendish, and told him what I wanted to do. He was really excited about it and we started to create some images together. The very first image I did had calla lilies in the foreground, as if I'd taken flowers out of their natural setting and put them into a studio setting. Really, they were fine art flower portraits. I couldn't quite relate to what I was doing, but my friend could already see it. It was coming from me, but I couldn't yet connect with it. Then I discovered this new piece of lighting equipment and bought an unusual lens that didn't have an aperture – a very soft-focusy sort of lens – and I ended up experimenting with a lighting/lens technique with long exposure and movement. I had discovered a new creative technique, using two pieces of equipment in a totally unconventional way. I created an amazing style and shot a series of single flowers against brightly-coloured backgrounds. They became so successful because I was using this technique that nobody had ever really seen before. It was vibrant and refreshing. Sadly, my friend died before he was able to see me achieve flower fame. I had created a unique style, which turned everything around for me and put me firmly on the map. The world exploded around me and I was suddenly in great demand!

What did you do with these early flower photos?

To begin with, everything I was doing was just for me because I had to create a body of new work to show people what I could do. I was in a very fortunate position as I was still working for the studio that I transitioned in. Then I was put in touch with an up and coming photographer's agent, Alan Wickes, who started to take my portfolio out and tout it around the advertising agencies.

I started to get small jobs to begin with, but in the whole area of advertising, packaging, design, publishing, editorial. It grew bit by bit and I became known: I became the specialist; the 'go to' photographer when someone wanted flowers in their campaign. My portfolio would be called in along with other people's and I started to work with some really big clients.

You've worked with high-level clients, including the Duchy of Cornwall. Who else have you worked with?

The biggest job I think I ever did was a one-day shoot for AT&T in America, a communications company. I was commissioned to do a shoot with dandelions with blowing seeds and it wasn't a time of year when dandelions were even growing! I had some challenging stuff to deal with in my career: people wanting things that didn't exist but telling me I was going to have to get it somehow. Which I did. I got something like £13,000 for that one-day shoot and it went on to make royalties and re-usage rights.

Swiss Life was another big client. They were doing a campaign with a white cross on a red background and they had an idea to use a particular image with a flower. Then, I started to work for packaging. Flowers can sell everything: I seemed to get into shooting a lot of flowers for teas, tissues, and sanitary towels. I did a whole paint range for Dulux. I worked for Waitrose, M&S, Boots, Mulberry, Barclays, Homebase, Superdrug, and Tesco – all the big-name companies.

Then one of my images got chosen by a design group called Carroll, Dempsey and Thirkell, who were one of the top five design groups in London in the 1980s. The Royal Horticultural Society Chelsea Flower Show was one of their clients and I got chosen for the show in 1997. It was a really big deal because the RHS had never used anything quite like that as an image on their advertising before. It was a turning point for everybody and that really raised my profile. It was a very abstract image of an oriental poppy and from that year onwards they started to use really arty advertising. I went on to do The Hampton Court Flower Show advertising and got a free ticket to Chelsea Flower Show every year after that! That was a real high point in my career.

I've done loads of book jackets, too, for publishers such as Time Warner Books, Macmillan, and Random House. It wasn't all flowers as I was a still life photographer as well. I tried my hand at food photography, but that didn't really work for me. Flowers identified who I was: they put me on the map. I really was one of the first people to go out there and do that particular type of photography. Then, I found that another woman, Carol Sharp, was also doing flowers but more plants and herbs. We were the two main women in London specialising in that area. Carol went on to create a photo library called Flowerphotos; she was looking for all the best flower images. I collaborated with her and put a lot of my imagery with her stock library because that was really big several years ago. It took over photography, really, because everybody started to go towards the libraries rather than commissioning. That's how the industry really started to change: people found the image first and then designed around it, as opposed to coming up with a concept and commissioning a photographer to create that image. A new era of stock photographers was born!

Tell me about your famous IKEA posters. How did they come about?

I did a series of six single flowers which really made my name and they were in demand. They were used for greeting cards by a company called Santoro Graphics and the company that worked with IKEA – called The Art Group – picked up on it and got in touch with me. They told me they would love to use two of my images for posters. I signed the contract and they wanted to have them as a pair. They'd been mounted and were ready to be framed. IKEA put them out together: just a yellow daffodil on a bright blue background and an orange gerbera on a turquoise background. That was it! They sold phenomenally well all over the world.

I'd been travelling and I remember being in Hong Kong one year and going into IKEA: seeing my work there was really crazy. Then, I was in Australia and went into IKEA and saw it there. After that, I remember one cold November evening being at my studio in London and I had a call from three friends that night saying they'd just seen my work on EastEnders. This is my claim to fame: those pictures had even found their way onto a set of EastEnders. It was hilarious! They had been put on the wall in the kitchen set of Ricky and Bianca, who spent most of their time rowing and fighting. There was my work in the background, creating a little haven of calm! It made me laugh and it was great because I ended up getting royalties. I remember getting the statements through monthly and seeing this unbelievable number of sales.

What were your defining moments?

One of my biggest goals was to own my own studio in London and have my own assistant working for me. I achieved this five years sooner than I ever thought I would.

At this point, I feel I have to share a great story as another defining moment, if not *the* defining moment for me. Very soon after I had landed in my first studio in Lant Street SE1, I received a phone call. At that particular time, I had created the series of single flowers on highly-coloured backgrounds – they were simple but very powerful. I had an exhibition with them on display at the AOP Gallery in London.

One day, I had a call out of the blue. The voice said in a very distinctive South African accent, "Hello, is Gill Orsman there?" I asked who was calling. "It's Barry Lategan here." I was thinking, "I know that name, but who is this?" I said, "Yes, hello, this is Gill speaking, how can I help you?" Barry said, "Hi Gill, I'm in a gallery in London and I've just seen your work ... I just wanted to call you to let you to know that: *You Have It!*"

Barry Lategan was hugely famous for fashion and portrait photography in London at that time, best known for his discovery of, and early work with, Twiggy. He has photographed Princess Anne, Paul McCartney, Linda McCartney, Iman, Germaine Greer, Calvin Klein, Margaret

Thatcher, Sol Campbell, John Major, and Salman Rushdie to name but a few.

Up until that call, I always answered my telephone with, “Hello, Studio. How can I help you?” Barry told me to answer my phone with, “Hello, this is Gill Orsman’s studio,” from then on.

I thanked him for the amazing accolade and put the phone down. Five minutes later, it rang again. I picked up the receiver and said, “Hello, Studio?” It was Barry again saying, “No! It’s Gill Orsman’s studio!” We laughed and chatted for a few more minutes, I thanked him again and we said goodbye. A few minutes later, the phone rang again and I thought, “Hmmn.” I picked up the phone and said, “Hello Gill Orsman’s studio, can I help you?” It was Barry Lategan again for the third and final time. All he said was, “That’s it – you got it!”, and hung up.

I never heard from him again, but it changed my whole demeanour. It gave me enormous confidence and a sense that I had finally been seen and acknowledged. I always answered the phone with my own name from that day forward.

What does your business do today?

I have been a photographer for over 30 years and I always imagined I would do this job to my very last dying day so the timing of this book comes at a very interesting juncture in my life. I no longer work as a flower photographer. After 25 years, I no longer have my studio as I gave this up.

I would say that the main reason I gave up my passion for photography was because of the onset of the digital age.

I had trained as a film photographer in every aspect of the craft. I absolutely loved working with large format cameras and the medium of film. There were so many different types of film I loved to work with and experiment with. One of my greatest loves was Polaroid Type 55. I had been taught well and I had become a master of my craft.

As the industry devoured the digital age with glee, bit by bit, I felt like my whole life was being dismantled, to the point where my favourite films were not even being made any more, let alone being processed in the labs. It really has been a slow and drawn out painful death! I have grieved this stage in my life long enough, together with many other photographers that I know. It was so grim that some of them even took their own lives!

We could write a whole chapter on this aspect of my life, but it's important to bring you up to date with the transition that I made at that time and am currently making today.

In 2001, I moved my home and business to Brighton. I was able to buy a converted old church hall as a live in/work space. I had always wanted a studio in my home and in an old church, so this was it. Moving from London to Brighton was a massive change for me. I got heavily into the art scene and was part of the Brighton Arts Festival every May for nine years running. I was part of the Artists' Open House trail and exhibited my work from my home/studio, along with other artists and craftspeople who I had invited to share my space with each year. Opening your home to the general public is a big deal for some people, but I loved it! It was very successful and I got to meet some amazing folk that just wandered into my home from off the street. This led to meeting new and interesting people, creating new working relationships and interesting commissions.

I had a remarkable experience about 10 years ago after I was invited to be part of a big charity event called 100 Artists for World AIDS Day. It was an auction event and I submitted one of my favourite pieces of work, now called 'The Sacred Heart.' It was one of my lesser-known flower images, originally commissioned by Swiss Life.

Up until that point you would never normally have seen me in front of the camera and that's just how I liked it – being unseen! But, on this occasion, a film school colleague had taken a picture of me standing next to my work, which was displayed on an easel. I was talking to a mother and her little girl.

Later on, when I received the image from my friend, I noticed a strange spherical object on the image in between my work and me. This caused me a great deal of curiosity as I had never seen anything like it before and I didn't know what it was at the time.

The following year I came across some information about orbs of light showing up in photos. I attended a talk by a lady called Diana Cooper, who works with angels and healing. I was astounded by what I learnt that night. She gave a slide show of orbs in photos and then I realised this must be what was next to me in that photo from the show. But what did it all mean?

The more fascinated I became with orbs, the more resistance I encountered when I tried to find out more. No one really knew what they were or wanted to admit that they actually existed at all. After Diana's talk, I decided that I would try and photograph orbs. Nothing really happened for ages, but after a while I seemed to get into the 'zone'. I started to capture some really unusual 'stuff'.

After a few years of experimenting and shooting at different locations, I started to notice that I had two orbs that kept showing up – around me! This started to get me thinking, "Is this just happening to me or does this happen to everyone?" It then became obvious for me to start doing some talks about orbs and share what I had found out. I even had some photographic references to show people.

I started my first talk at a Holistic Fair in Steyning in 2012. Having never done a public talk before, I was absolutely terrified as loads of people turned up. There was a real interest in this subject and I found out that quite a lot of people had heard of orbs already.

After that, I captured one of the best photos of an orb I had ever taken so far. I was at the Lewes bonfire parade. I'd never been before and I'd heard so much about it. It was completely crazy: burning effigies in the street and letting off bangers, a real health and safety nightmare! I was at this fantastic, huge bonfire piled up with pallets about 100 feet high. The fireworks lit up the night sky. I kept photographing the stages of the bonfire as it burnt down throughout the evening. Towards the end, I did a shot of the huge bonfire, now reducing to ashes, and captured what looked like the full moon above these raging flames. It took my breath away. I'd never seen anything like it. I said out loud, "Wow! That's the money shot!"

The following year a friend sent me a link to an international photography competition I had never heard of before. I entered the orb image (now called 'The Phoenix Orb') into the competition as the theme was 'Beauty of Light'

The Crown Prince of Dubai sponsored the competition and I was sent an invite to go to the awards ceremony in the financial district of Dubai. I didn't know at the time if I had won or if I was even a runner up. But I went along and experienced the whole awards ceremony. It was incredible: 10 times better than the Oscars! They had 26,000 entries so I guessed I must have been high on the shortlist to even get the invite. We all received a Polaroid camera as a gift from the Prince with his name embossed in gold along the box: *Hamdan Bin Mohammed Bin Rashid Al Maktoum – International Photography Awards*. That has been another defining moment on the next part of my journey with orbs!

Later that year, in 2013, I decided I was going to start running workshops teaching people how to photograph orbs. I knew this had never been done before, or at least not in the UK.

I do believe it is the start of what I am really here to do: this is really pushing the boundaries and delving into the realms of the unseen. I have coined the phrase ‘Seeing the Unseen’.

I feel like I'm at the beginning of a new journey: I feel very much that I'm a messenger for this. I've been told in the past that I'm going to be photographing much more than orbs; that other things will be revealed to me. And it’s true – they are! It's almost as if I'm here to show the world something and I'm going to be able to bring some sort of understanding or message whilst working with the orbs. I'm still in the early stages of trying to work out what orbs really are and, to be honest, nobody really knows what they are or what they mean. A lot of people have their own opinions but where I sit with it personally, at the moment, is that I think they're guardian angel spirit energy, and I have now photographed my two beautiful guardian angels.

There's a realm that we can't see because we have a limited visible spectrum and it's just off the edge of that spectrum. The digital era has created highly-sophisticated technology that lets us see into this realm with the aid of infrared sensors. I've learnt a lot about why they're showing up and I've started running workshops, teaching other people how to photograph orbs, with 1-to-1 sessions and in groups, at home and abroad.

Because of this fascinating journey, I have started writing my first book about orbs and I am currently looking for the right publisher. It is my intention to make a movie about this subject and to raise the awareness for this exciting new phenomenon. To be continued...!

What advice do you have for anyone else wanting to achieve a similar level of success?

It's all about going for what you love. Listen with your heart – be led by your heart, not led by your mind – and don't be swayed by others' opinions. When you find what you love to do, it will never feel like work. Surround yourself with positive people who can support your vision and encourage you to go for it!

Just remember the universe has your back and you came here to deliver your unique gift to the world and we will all be better off when you have shared and delivered what you came here to do. Never underestimate yourself and never give up!

Intuition is a really big gift, but it's so subtle – you go with the gut reaction, but then you go into your mind and listen to people and think, "Oh, don't be so ridiculous. You can't possibly do that." But if you dare to go there, that realm is where the magic of life actually opens up. A friend calls it 'betwixt and between'. Get a good coach to guide you; the world is now full of them. Find your own tribe who's going to support your journey, and don't give up; just keep going. I believe that if you're here right now, you've chosen to be here for a reason. You've chosen to come here to deliver something very valuable and necessary. Just keep believing in yourself and you will create a life beyond your wildest dreams.

LISA ORME

"At junior school, the teachers told my mum and dad that I would never amount to much ... little did they know!"

Job Title: Managing Director of Keys Mortgages and Landlord/Developer/Inventor

Bio: Property Finance Consultant specialising in buy-to-let, HMO, bridging, commercial and development finance, and we love complex and unusual cases! Twenty years' experience in the property industry as a developer, investor, and landlord, with a large portfolio of properties in the Midlands.

Services: Keys is fully regulated by the FCA, and as specialist mortgage advisers we offer all types of mortgages, second charge loans, commercial and bridging loans for residential purposes, property investment and development. That means that we can offer you a true one-stop shop for all your property finance needs! We are based in Coventry but work with clients remotely anywhere in the world. We've developed systems that enable you to get on with your life and let us do what we do best!

Awards and Honours: Financial Times Top 25 UK Female Financial Adviser; Best Specialist Lending Adviser Finalist – National Mortgage Adviser Awards.

Contact:

E: enquiries@keys-mortgages.com

P: 02476 455 445

Website: www.keys-mortgages.com

♦ ♦ ♦

I wanted to be an airline pilot as far back as I can remember. I went to a brilliant girls' grammar school where they were very encouraging of girls who wanted to go into male-oriented careers. We didn't play any girly sports; we played cricket because the headmistress loved it. The school really encouraged girls to try for male-dominated roles and I was accepted for a sponsorship with British Airways and then turned down at the medical for being a quarter of an inch too short.

Although there is no height limit now, there was back then in the 1980s. I was applying to be a commercial pilot – there was no way I could have afforded to do it without a sponsorship, so not getting it was gutting. The school tried to encourage me to go into aeronautical engineering and I was accepted by the only three universities that offered it at the time. The universities were very keen to get women on to their courses too. But if couldn't fly airplanes, I didn't really want to make them. So, I didn't know what to do.

My aunt loved reading about real crimes and gave me some books, a couple of which were about early pathology and early forensic scientists like Bernard Spilsbury and Keith Simpson. I found it absolutely fascinating. I used to read these books as a hobby – I wasn't playing with Sindy, I was reading murder books. A nice normal childhood! Then something happened which was really weird.

To me, forensic science wasn't anything you went into as a career; I thought boffins did that type of job because that's what I'd been reading. Anyway, I wasn't going to be a pilot, I'd decided I didn't want to do aeronautical engineering and I didn't know what I was going to do. I went into the library, got out *The A-Z of Careers*, sat there feeling pretty sorry for myself and opened up the book. It opened on F for Forensic Scientist. TV programmes like CSI have made the whole field more popular, but back then nobody really knew what they were. So, I read it because I knew what a forensic scientist was, whereas most people wouldn't have at the time.

I realised that I'd got the qualifications that would allow me to become an assistant forensic scientist as I'd studied all the sciences and maths when I was aiming at being a pilot or studying engineering, so I applied. There were six labs around the country and I was offered jobs at three. So, just turned 19, with my little car, my suitcase, and two budgies, off I trotted to Huntingdon in Cambridgeshire and I started working as a forensic scientist in the lab there. Once you're in, it's a typical civil service arrangement – you can move around. I worked there for a little over a year until I started feeling homesick and thinking I'd really like to move to the Birmingham lab. They said, "Sure, we've got a vacancy there." So, I moved back to Brum and continued working there for another 12 years.

About a year before I left, the Forensic Science Service had asked me and some others to take part in biometric testing that our HR department was introducing. The lady who was doing all the testing went through all these results and told me I was really unusual. She said, "You don't have the mind of a scientist; you're very creative." I think left brain is creative and right brain's logical and according to her, I was really over on the left brain, which you rarely see in the science world, but you often find among self-employed people and entrepreneurs. She asked me if I had ever thought of starting my own business.

This was all going somewhere, as I discovered later, though at the time I thought it was weird. I told her that I hadn't thought of starting my own business and she said, "Well, that's where you belong; your brain's not cut out for logic and science and things like that." Then, lo and behold, it turned out she was an Amway rep in her spare time, doing multi-level marketing, and she asked me if I would be interested in it.

I'd never heard of it but my husband, Stuart had, and he told me about multi-level marketing and pyramid selling and so on. I listened to what he was saying and even though I'd never entertained the thought of being self-employed, I thought, "Well, why not give it a go?" That was the first time I ever read a motivational book, because Amway is very into that type of thing. We went to lots of motivational events and although selling the products was of less interest, I really enjoyed the motivational side of it. We heard some fantastic speakers over the year or so we were there. At one of the events, in 2000, I picked up the book *Rich Dad, Poor Dad* by Robert Kyosaki, and as we were due to go to Australia for a long holiday I chucked it in my suitcase.

We were on holiday for six weeks and on the last week, I decided to take the book to the jacuzzi and read it there. I couldn't put it down. With hindsight, I realise it was actually all about network marketing: telling people that if they wanted to start their own business for a hundred dollars, then network marketing was the ideal way to do it.

The strange thing is, though, that what I read in that book was *property*. Stuart was a telecoms engineer. He was travelling all over the country and overseas. After 13 years in the Forensic Science Service, I was now travelling up and down the country training police officers in crime scene management and he and I were like passing ships in the night. I thought, "I don't want to do this for the next forty years." We'd talked about doing something together, but what were a telecoms engineer and a forensic scientist ever going to do together? What sort of a business is that?

That was why I picked up on property. We'd both been interested in property because we'd always wanted to build our own home. We used to go out and look at show homes and go to the build shows and I started wondering if that might be an option for us. I did not know a single person in my entire family or among my friends who owned anything other than their own home. I didn't even know buy-to-let existed or that you could rent properties out – I didn't know anybody who did that. But I went running in to Stuart and said, "You need to read this book right now!"

He was the same, he couldn't put it down, and we spent the rest of our holiday making plans. We didn't know exactly what the plans were, but we were determined we were going to create our own business and become self-employed and self-sufficient. I didn't want to rely on a government pension and we'd got next-to-no pension anyway, and I just wanted better for us. If nothing else, I wanted us to not be passing ships in the night; I wanted us to work together and be together.

We picked up our car in the UK and stopped at the petrol station and saw an *Exchange and Mart* and a *Dalton's Weekly.* Both of them have 'Homes', 'Property', 'Businesses', and so forth at the top. I picked up both of them, came home, unpacked, sat down, went through them and found an advert for a company called Southcourt.

A man named Mike Hathaway set up Southcourt in the 1980s or 1990s and used to run a letting agency. What he did was this: he took his manual on how to run a letting agency, put it into an A4 folder and sold it for £200. I thought, "That's property. That's a business." It seemed like a good start so I ordered it and read it, and within a couple of weeks of coming back from holiday, I'd set up our own letting agency.

God, that was hard work! It wasn't me at all – I didn't enjoy it and I didn't like it. But the funny thing is that Graham Hathaway, whose dad set up Southcourt, is now one of my mortgage clients, twenty years on. Which is amazing! It's really strange how these things all come full circle. I've been recommending Southcourt for years, telling clients to buy the same pack I bought because it's a fantastic introduction to being a landlord. You don't have to run a letting agency, but everything you need is in there.

In the meantime, I had started working for a boss I didn't get along with at the Forensic Science Service. I started to feel physically sick, miserable, and almost suicidal in a job that I adored, to the point where I just couldn't face going in each day. One morning, I was sitting there in the kitchen at home with Stuart and I said, "I don't think I can walk through the door." He said, "If it's making you feel that bad, don't go in." So that was it: I walked out of my job.

I soon realised being a letting agent wasn't what I wanted to do either, though, and that the people that were actually making the money were the landlords and not the ones that were managing their property for a tenner a month. So, we sat down, looked at our finances – what we'd done and what we'd got – and asked ourselves if we were going to make a go of this new business or not. What was the worst that could happen? We cashed in our endowment just before the bottom fell out of that market, bought a three-bed semi- that needed a lot of work, renovated it from top to bottom, sold it and doubled our money.

We raised £30,000 by selling the endowment and by the time we'd sold that property we'd got £60,000. So, we repeated the whole process a couple of times and made some more money.

We bought and sold inside a timescale of about six to nine months. During that time, I earned about the same as I earned for the whole year in my old job. We were renovating a property in our spare time, using a builder, and we really enjoyed it. I'd been putting the word out round the new local developments and after we'd done a few more renovations I was contacted by a builder who was a site manager at King's Oak, which was part of Barratt's at the time. He told me they'd just had an investor let them down on four houses and said if we could complete before the end of the month, for year end – we'd got less than two weeks – he'd let us have them at the original price even though they were already worth £25,000 more each. Carpets, curtains, light fittings – it was all on offer, and they'd even pay our stamp duty.

I was determined to make it happen no matter what and that was the start of our portfolio. We bought those four houses in 2002 and ironically the market then was more like it is now: you couldn't refinance straight away, you had to wait six months, lenders were all over you like a rash to check your background, income, and everything else. There was none of the free-and-easy lending that came along a couple of years later. We managed to pull it off and got our first four buy-to-lets. Then we waited, did another couple of refurbs, made some money from that, waited another nine months or so and refinanced the first two buy-to-lets we'd bought, pulled out our money and off we went again.

We did that for a year or so, until about 2004, when the market went mad. Everybody knows what it was like for about four or five years. We'd set out just wanting to make an income so that we could work for ourselves and have a nice pension; that was all we wanted. But before we knew it, we were doing three or four deals a week. It was insane! We had so many deals on, we were just buying places and reselling them within a week without doing anything to them and ended up making a profit. It was crazy, just picking stuff up for £100,000, negotiating and reselling it for £125,000 a week later. Sometimes we retained places if it made sense.

We were building a big portfolio, making a lot of money from buying and selling. In 2007, we decided to get married and we went back to Australia for eight weeks for our honeymoon. Both of us had packed in our jobs by then and gone full-time in property. For five years, we'd been doing hundreds of deals – new builds, conversions, straight buy, and sell – we'd built up a massive portfolio of properties across the Midlands and we'd been riding the market. It was just luck and good timing.

On our honeymoon in October/November 2007, we sat down and discussed what the next phase of our life should be. Both of us decided that though it had all been fun, we'd had enough. Property wasn't really for us – we'd just ended up in the business. We decided that what we really liked was the buy and sell, doing the deals. We really did not like being landlords at all. We decided that we were going to come back, sell off the portfolio, do some buy and sell and go and build our own house. We didn't know the crash was just around the corner!

We came back in early 2008 to find the whole world was falling apart financially. I'd always said, as a property investor, that it didn't matter if the market was going up or down, you'd make money. What I'd never, ever realised or expected was what happens if the market's static. We weren't falling off a cliff, like people were suggesting. It was worse than that: it was static. There was no financing, there was hardly any lending, people weren't buying and they weren't selling – and you can only make money if there are transactions going on. It was dead for about 18 months. There was just nothing happening, and that was the hard bit.

So that put paid to the ideas we'd dreamt up in Australia and for eighteen months we just consolidated. Stuart was quite happy to play golf, but I was itching to do something else! The irony was, I was minutes away from setting up a property and crime-scene cleaning business. I'd worked in crime scenes when I was in forensic science and I thought, "Well, I'll certainly have the contacts. I can always dip back into those, cleaning up crime scenes and things like that." And it overlapped with the property side: if you have a look at some repossessed properties, they even look like crime scenes! So, I'd decided that was going to be my next venture and I had it all planned out. I'd even got the graphics; all my brochures were ready to go.

I was brainstorming some ideas when our builder came in, who was building a house for us in Rugby. "What's all this about?" he said. I told him it was my new business venture; I was bored and wanted to get my teeth into something else. Totally out of the blue, he said, "You'd make a really good mortgage broker." I'd never considered it – it hadn't even crossed my radar. "Why do you think that?" I asked. "You're brilliant at problem-solving," he said. "You love numbers, and I just think it'd be something you're really good at. You should look into it." He asked me if I would like to sort out his mortgage for him instead of his usual broker. So, I sat down with him and went through all his numbers – just the general data – and he said, "See, I told you! You're not even a mortgage broker and you know what you're talking about. You've done so many mortgages of your own."

Stuart and I both decided to do the exams. We studied in our spare time and both passed. I then spoke to the mortgage broker I was using myself at the time and told him I was thinking about becoming a broker but was still going to use him. "I think that's a great idea," he said. "Why don't you go into business with me?" What he wanted was to be able to concentrate on the more interesting specialist areas and for me to take on what he called his 'vanilla stuff' and fit that around the property business. This suited me fine. We were all set to go ahead and then, unexpectedly, he phoned me up and said he'd changed his mind and was going to go off and run a pub. "The business is yours!" he said.

In 2008 and 2009, all I got were calls from people asking if they could still get a self-certified mortgage. "I'm showing £10,000 income and I want to borrow a million – I can't do that any more?" To which I had to say, "No. Afraid not." My first six months of calls were from people like that. It was still the time of the credit crunch and people were desperate and couldn't go anywhere and nobody was lending. I thought, "Hmm, this isn't really panning out as I expected." As I had nobody to ask for advice, I went back to my usual thing, which is social media. I found a discussion forum for brokers online, joined, started chatting with people and got in touch with a really lovely guy in Wales who I'm still friends with. He gave me loads of tips and told me to change my support network. I'm now directly authorised, but at the time I was in a mortgage broker network.

Of course, I was really well-known in property circles in social media. Somebody said to me, "I didn't know you were a broker." I thought, "Well, I've been a broker for two years; clearly I'm not getting the message out." I started switching my social media posts. Instead of answering the 'being a landlord' posts, I just answered the 'mortgage' posts and that opened the floodgates. I got more and more business and realised what I actually loved doing was specialist cases. We'll do anything, we'll take anybody at all; if they want a mortgage or a secured loan, we'll do it. But I love the problem cases – the problem-solving.

What I realise is that for my entire life I've loved problem-solving. My favourite game as a kid was Cluedo. You speak to any property investor and they'll tell you their favourite game as a kid was Monopoly. Speak to a doctor, it was Operation. Mine was Cluedo. I love problem-solving, I really do. I'd done it as a forensic scientist because that's what the whole job is about, and what I loved about property wasn't being a landlord or developing, it was problem-solving. Now, as a mortgage broker, I get to do that every single day. I spend my whole day solving other people's problems, finding a route, finding a way, looking at things differently. What's not to love?

Stuart also invented a new security product – Letterblox – which we developed and patented and are now looking at licensing to a European company. You never know what is around the corner!

So that was how I went from pilot to forensic scientist to property investor and developer to mortgage broker and inventor. It just happened and to me it just seems natural, but everybody else thinks it's strange. I absolutely love it. I feel like I've got as close to the perfect life as you can get.

How did you come to be named as one of the top 25 financial advisors by The Financial Times?

It's the one award I'm really, really proud of because I was nominated by someone else. I know a lot of back-scratching goes on with awards, a lot of nepotism. So, what I loved about the FT award was that I was actually nominated by the network I used to work in as a broker. They put me forward with a whole spiel about me, saying I was allowed to do lots of specialist cases and work with commercial lenders and bridging lenders, whereas nearly all the other brokers were not allowed to do that.

I'd got a good relationship with lenders and was building up all these specialist relationships, which my network allowed me to carry on. But what was a real win was that social media was coming to the fore. It's amazing how we all take for granted Facebook and Twitter and so on, but they are incredibly new. Even the term 'social media' is only a couple of years old.

I was on property discussion forums back in 2000, but social media is new, the networks are scared stiff of regulation, and the regulators aren't keen on social media – so the networks told us we couldn't have a business profile on Facebook or Twitter; that we couldn't tweet about products or lenders or rates or anything. They were scared of it.

To be fair, the network that I worked with decided to look into it a little more to see if the fear was justified. They were wondering whether there was a way to work with social media because it's so significant and so many of their brokers wanted to use it. Because I was known to social media, they got in touch with me and asked me to help them write their strategy.

I got in touch with a couple of other guys who I knew were keen on social media profiles and a group of us got together and wrote their whole social media policy. They were one of the first networks to embrace social media and get the message out to brokers they were welcome to use it if they wanted to, whereas a lot of networks remained scared of it all and didn't want their brokers using it.

It was really refreshing, and it got them a lot of kudos and we got a lot of press as a result. The next thing I knew was that I was being contacted by the FT to tell me I'd been nominated by the network for their annual top female advisers' award.

They asked me a bit about myself and I had to put a CV together, but most of it had been done by the network. There are women at the top of the list that run major IFA organisations with thousands of staff, really well-known in the industry. They told me I was number 24 on the list. I didn't have any staff. I was a sole broker, sole adviser, sole business owner. So just to be in the top 25 and have been nominated by somebody else was incredible and, yes, a very, very proud moment.

What are your defining moments; the things that have helped you move forward over the years?

Firstly, people might say "Oh, it's alright for you", but I wasn't born with a silver spoon in my mouth.

I was born and raised in a council house in Birmingham with my mum, my dad, my brother, and my nan. I went to an ordinary school just down the road. My dad was a decorator and worked for the council, my mum worked in a factory and my nan looked after us. My mum and dad were lucky enough to be able to buy their council house with the help of my nan, for the princely sum of £9,000. We had a little car and we went down to Cornwall once a year for a two-week holiday, but we never felt we went without.

I had a wonderful childhood; my parents are still with us and they're fantastic. I can't look back on anything about my childhood with any unhappiness at all, and my parents allowed me to be very independent from a very young age, which gave me a lot of strength.

Everything I've done or achieved has come from sheer determination and not giving in. I wasn't handed anything on a plate.

At junior school, the teachers told my mum and dad that I would never amount to much, so not to expect too much of me. I didn't know that at the time, but I ended up going into the top set at a girls' grammar school – so, little did they know! If I want something, I become fixated on achieving it to the point you'd literally have to break my legs to stop me. The flipside is that I'm also very flexible, and if it doesn't happen I realise it wasn't meant to be. I push and push and push and push if I'm sure something is the right thing, but if the universe keeps pushing back, I stop and listen and think, "Maybe it's actually not meant to be." I see where else it's taking me and nine times out of ten, it's taken me somewhere better.

Twice we've lost a huge amount of money – really an eye-watering amount of money. One was a business deal that went bad and another was a property venture that went bad. People can look in from the outside and think everything's always gone well for me, but actually it hasn't.

On both occasions, I could have sat there and thrown in the towel and declared bankruptcy – and that was even before we got to the credit crunch, which was a scary, scary time as a property investor. But I have always had this attitude of one day at a time. What else are you going to do? You just get up and you keep going and keep going and hope that one day it will turn and eventually it does. You just chalk it up and decide either you're going to wallow or you're going to pick yourself up, dust yourself off and get on with it. We're now in a better place than we've ever been, life-wise, family-wise, business-wise, money-wise, despite everything that's happened. You could say *because* of everything that's happened. It depends which way you look at it.

So, coming back to aha moments, I think one would definitely be reading *Rich Dad, Poor Dad* because that took me from being an employee to being self-employed. Even though we'd started with the property, I knew it was very volatile and I was the major income earner. We'd got a mortgage, kids, cars, and so on, and then Stuart told me to walk out of my job because I was unhappy... Talk about a baptism of fire! Two weeks after I walked out of that job, Stuart got a letter from his employer of nearly twenty years saying, sorry to tell you, the company's gone bust, can you please return your car. So, within two weeks, we'd gone from two seriously good incomes coming in to nil.

So, we had to make it work. When I think of all the things we've done and achieved, it's not building houses or getting planning permission round sites, it's the fact that for near on 20 years, I've been self-employed and I've always been able to make money no matter what's been thrown at me. I think that's the thing that I feel most proud of.

What are the personal beliefs that have sustained you through the challenging times?

We're both lucky: we both had really good upbringings with a steady family. My parents are absolutely wonderful. I used to look at my mum and dad and think, "If only I could have that relationship: how close they are, absolute best friends." And I can categorically say that my relationship with Stuart is even better. Growing up with that example of a great relationship, and saying "I want that or nothing" was always a big influence. I just love and worship my dad. He makes me laugh and we've got a very similar sense of humour, which is wicked. But he's also very placid and calm. He and Stuart are like two peas in a pod. So, I've got a great relationship with somebody that I dote on and who dotes on me, which is a big influence.

I think one of the things that I would really like to get across is the importance of contentment. I use that word all the time now. I ran two big events a couple of years ago, in London, and I wanted a motivational speaker and thought of someone called Brad Burton. Then it occurred to me that I'd booked him for my event but I'd never heard him talk. So he invited me to his one-day Brad Camp, as he calls it, which is about finding your why?, your what next?, and your what do I do now? The boot camp was a bit of fun and I joined in as I always will, and I was thinking that I'd got a few hints and tips and he was a nice guy, not like your normal motivational speaker at all.

Then, late afternoon, all of a sudden something clicked. That was the absolute best aha moment I've ever had in my life. It was life changing. As you start identifying what you really want at this boot camp, you fill in a little book with drawings and other things. Everybody says the same thing: *I want a big house, and I want a couple of nice cars and I want holidays and I want to give to charity*. Because we're all taught the same things. I saw a great quote once. "*Most people think they want financial freedom and yet don't know what to do with themselves on a rainy Sunday afternoon.*" I love that quote because it's so true. If you're in property, everybody talks about wanting financial freedom and being able to do what they want when they want – but actually, most of us would be bored stiff within a week.

So, it's about finding what you want to do with your time. That was a big aha moment when I realised I don't want to pack in work. It was as if I was in a trance. All of a sudden, I wrote: *I don't want to work Fridays and Mondays.* I'd never, ever thought like that before. It had never crossed my mind that actually I love what I do and I like working and I don't want to not work, but I hate Mondays and I hate Fridays. I love to have Fridays off and I love weekends, and who likes Mondays? You still get that kid thing, I think, on a Sunday night when you think, "Oh, back to work tomorrow," no matter how much you love your job. So, I decided that's what I fancied: having Fridays and Mondays off. Not always, but on a regular basis, and that suddenly became my focus. If I could find a way to have more Fridays and Mondays off, how perfect would that be?

So, again, the universe, gods, I don't know what, took a hand. We needed some legal advice and at the solicitor's, I met a lady called Amy and I fell in love with her straight away. I was really stressed at the time and she just handled me beautifully. I thought, "I want her working for me", and I gave her a business card and told her if she ever decided to get out of law and into mortgages, to let me know. She phoned that night and two weeks later she came and joined me and my niece, Cheryl, who was already working for me.

Cheryl and Amy now pretty much run everything and, ironically, I'm now doing what I love. We're about to launch a podcast. I'm writing articles, and I'm sure I'll get round to writing my books. I spend the time I want to with clients and on the phone solving problems, then I pass it all over to Cheryl and Amy to finish the job.

I also bought a caravan and I love the peace and quiet that gives us; I can stay in touch with clients and the office but get plenty of Mondays and Fridays off!

The one word that I put all that down to is contentment. You just need to find out what it is that you love doing and position your life to create that for you. I get to spend my days problem-solving, and I've got brilliant staff that support me in doing that, and Stuart and I travel and we have a great life. If I want to knock off at one o'clock and go swimming for the afternoon, I can.

What is your advice for anyone else wanting to achieve what you have?

I think the main thing for people that are reading this, male or female, is about being flexible and open. When the exams come around, all the parents go on Facebook to say that their kids have got a 2:1 or six A*s, but what about the poor kids that haven't got what they expected? It doesn't matter, it was meant to be – trust me, life has a better plan for you!

I also want to reach out to all the business people that have had five businesses and every single one has gone bust, and they think they can't do it any more. I think that you just have to keep going and you've just got to find your thing, which is not necessarily what you think it is. It doesn't matter if you don't go to university. It doesn't matter if your dream job doesn't come true – trust me, life has a better plan for you.

I wanted to be an airline pilot and, knowing myself as well as I do now, I know I would hate it. I've had businesses that haven't worked out, I've had property deals that have gone wrong and lost money, but I'm still exactly where I want to be and extremely contented and happy with my life. So, don't give in. Be flexible. Something better is waiting for you. Right now, it might not feel like it, but it is.

BERNADETTE ANA BRUCKNER, MA PHD.C.

"It doesn't matter what challenges my clients have. My deepest belief is that we will find a solution and that they will feel better afterwards."

Job title: Intuitive mentor in business, health, education. Senior tool/programme designer for resilience methods. Author and intern. Speaker.

Bio: A creative all-rounder who has worked successfully in different fields in Austria and abroad. Through her interest in corporate communications, marketing, human resources, and other areas of business, she has accumulated an enormous amount of knowledge over the last 30 years.

Educated by top international trainers, including Richard Bandler, Robert Dilts, Roy Martina, Eric Pearl, Mark Anastasi, and Clinton Swaine.

Internationally active as a holistic trainer in health, nutrition, and mental health, specialising in exceptional methods which are 'non-box-thinking'.

Founder of 'Intuitive Coaching/Therapy', advanced energetical development of NLP with '1-minute coaching-to-go', as well as 'ORINITION® – n(fl)ourish soul.mind.body.' – an innovative nutrition work of remembering our own body intelligence.

Master's degree in health management in tourism with a focus on public health, nutrition, and sport. International PhD and research in the fields of health communication and linguistic science, with focus on psycho-linguistics, as well as health promotion and neuro-plasticity. Second master studies in business leadership with focus on HR, organizational development, and strategy.

Business: Health-in-All Mentoring

Services:

'Intuitive Coaching for Coaches and Therapists' workshop.

'Orinition Nutrition Work' workshop for nutrition trainers, dieticians, and nutrition scientists.

'Being Inconceivable ME' power day/s for women, mums, mumpreneurs learning about the female intuition deep within.

Tools for the female intuition in business.

1-to-1 coaching/mentoring in business and holistic health.

In the future: nurturing / accompanying of cancer patients, clients with Asperger's, and mumpreneurs.

Contact:

E: ana@orinition.com or brucknercb@gmx.at

Website: www.health-in-all.com and www.orinition.com

♦ ♦ ♦

I grew up in a bakery and as far as I can remember I was always helping my mother. It's like the saying, 'You always want to do what your mother does.' So I served and I was in the bakery helping out. I rarely saw my father because he was sleeping during the day and working at night. Sometimes I just woke up in the night and went into the bakery in order to see him. It was really hard work, but I really learned a lot from it. Right up until this day, it doesn't matter where I am, I will always survive because I learned the value of hard work very early on. I took care of everyone in my family. We barely had any holidays, but I got everything that I wanted.

Since I was a child, I've always had a Leo attitude. I was like a lion that roared and everyone would listen to me; I was the centre of attention. I trusted everyone and trusted that everything would work out well for me. I was someone who loved to be independent, instead of waiting for someone else to look after me. My father began paying me to help in the bakery around the age of ten, so I thrived on having my own money and being able to afford everything I wanted, without relying on anyone else.

I'm a Fire Dragon in the Chinese horoscope. I've had the attitude of a leader since I was just a child. I listen to myself, rather than to others. I learned to be very tough growing up, but I was still there for everyone else and caring for them. I've continued doing that in all companies where I have worked over the years.

I'm pretty sure that's the reason why I ended up creating my own sport coaching and nutrition coaching and also emergency resilience tools. This work ethic is in my blood: not just taking care of me, but also taking care of others. That's something I really learned from my family.

What did you do after you left your family bakery?

I worked in industry at a top level, building up subsidiaries and international sales. Most of the time, my work was in fields that I didn't have much knowledge of. The feeling was, 'You've been selling so well in your bakery, so I want you to work for me building up international sales.' I had a month's training and then I was in France building up sales in fields that I knew little about. I was 20, I was young for what I was doing, but they had so much faith in me. Their attitude was very much, 'Either she sinks or she swims'. So I needed to learn as quickly as possible. I am happy that I grew up so tough, otherwise I would have sunk again and again. Instead, I was able to swim. I learned so fast that within one year I was better than someone who had worked there 20 years. I could talk with those men at the top management level without being fazed by it. I was able to speak confidently and knowledgeably about everything that was going on. They confided in me and shared strategies that they didn't discuss with anyone else.

I have the CV of a 60-year-old person because I learnt so fast. I knew the company better than it knew itself, I think. I've worked in big companies and in small companies. I always checked in with every single branch to get a feel for them. I get a feeling about who I really can learn something from. Back then, they talked with me only in French and refused to talk to me in English. My French was not that good so I needed to learn the language as fast as possible, in addition to everything else. My challenges were really good as life lessons. As a woman in a male-dominated industry, you can only be taken seriously when you have a high level of knowledge, so I had to learn quickly.

In general, I have been focusing throughout my career on public health, nutrition, and sport.

The lessons I've learned have formed the basis of what I do today. It's also enabled me to create business tools for female leadership. How to be taken seriously when you are a good-looking woman and how to avoid that feeling of, 'You need to sleep with the boss to get ahead.' It took me a lot of time and different companies to really get to a better place. I want to help other women to shortcut those problems so that they don't get compromised.

What were the defining moments in your life that helped your business to move forward?

The bankruptcy of our family bakery in 2009 was a defining moment. Before this, I always knew that I had a safety net: I had a job to go back to if I wanted. I knew everything about the bakery; I was also a sales manager there in the early days of my career. It was my family's whole world.

The bankruptcy was devastating – it was so hard to let go of something that my father and my grandfather built up. I quit a really good job in Vienna in order to help my family through the bankruptcy because it was a really tough time for them. My father was in hospital so it felt like my whole world broke apart from one day to the next. But when you have a leader role, you don't have time to think about anything other than being in the moment. I checked on everyone to make sure that they were alright and could handle everything that was happening. It was like being a quiet hole in the middle of a huge hurricane and being there for everyone else.

Around the same time, I spent ten days in London with Richard Bandler for the Master NLP (Neuro-Linguistic Programming) practitioner programme.

I'm so happy I did that. This was a defining moment, when I understood what was really important in my life. After the ten days, I changed my friendship group because my old friends just didn't fit me any more. I changed my clothes – I just threw everything away – because I realised that I had to nurture myself and my family to avoid burnout and breakdown. I thought, "Okay, this stuff is happening in this moment, but what can I change, and how can I be truly in my full power and nurture my whole family?"

I had always looked up to my brother; he was always strong and he didn't take many things too emotionally. But he lost everything during the bankruptcy and I had to really keep an eye on him to make sure that he stayed on an even keel. It took around seven years in order to pay everything back after the bankruptcy. It was really, really tough.

During this time, I took a sabbatical not only to nurture my family but also to make space for myself so I could reflect on what I wanted to do with my life. Because, as Mother Theresa said, "Go home and love your family if you want to change the world." I couldn't go back to top management level when my family was suffering. A high-paying job was not worth it in comparison. I was also feeling suicidal because I had no idea how to solve the problems. I had had a Speedy Gonzales career and a good life, but it was only good because of my family.

During this time, I was taking care of three of my aunts. They were war children and they did a lot of hard work, but they never nurtured themselves as they were always there for everyone else. So, I was childminding and I was also doing terminal care. My experiences became the foundation for much of the coaching work I do today. What I see the most when coaching a lot of people, especially women and mumpreneurs, is that we forget to really, truly live. Most of the time, it's like we are almost dead. We don't go after our dreams or live our lives in alignment with what's important to us.

Another significant event that really woke me up was a car accident I had. I got hit by a truck and my car was totally smashed up. I was driving on the motorway and passing by a truck when something happened and I was suddenly spinning around at 140km per hour. The whole car was broken on the side. I had nothing to protect me, yet I got out of the car without a scratch. Nothing. It was shocking. I just walked away from that accident. It was amazing that I was still alive. I remember thinking, "What the hell happened here?" The only thing that I perceived – because I'm very intuitive and I really believe in living in alignment with my guides – is that they were saying to me, "You should be dead by now. Something is wrong here. You need to go to another way."

I remember thinking, "Woah. Okay." I had two other strange accidents where I really felt that I had survived when I shouldn't be alive any more. So I concluded that something was telling me to get on a different path. I truly believe in free will, but also that there is something out there that is guiding you. You read a lot about people having near-death experiences and they often change their whole life or choose an entirely different path. That's how it was for me. The car accident was like a sign for me to change what I was doing.

The next step was for me to start projects in the health and social field, offering a free service to help others. I wanted to help other people who were suffering to reclaim their full power and feel in control again.

What does your business do? Who do you help?

The main areas of my work are:

Creating resilience methods for different groups like people with Asperger's and learning difficulties, soldiers, mumpreneurs and women managers, cancer patients, people dealing with crises and trauma. I also did a PhD to explain scientifically – with neuroscience, psycholinguistics and language/ communication science – why my tools are working.

Intuitive coaching in business, health, and education, one-to-one with CEOs, mumpreneurs, and top managers. This includes teaching emergency tools: time management tools and decision-making tools, based on using our own wisdom and the intuition of the subconsciousness.

Nutrition mentoring and my own nutrition work.

I help a lot of people who have a beautiful vision, but who have no idea how to bring it about. So I bring all my business knowledge to them because it's really fun to help people fulfil their dreams. I created different resilience tools, my own intuitive coaching, and my own intuitive nutrition programme.

Sometimes, you get this feeling inside: all these dreams and visions are appearing before you, but you are too shy to reach out for them. I'm actually quite an introverted person myself. But I have a lot of friends who introduce me to other people or who take me to places that teach me not to be an introvert any more. It's like the universe smacks me and says, "No, this is not the right way. Just listen!" These moments are like getting a wake-up call from the universe, but a lot of people don't listen to it like I do.

How did you develop the resilience methods that you use to help your clients?

I've been developing these resilience methods for over 20 years. But since the bankruptcy, I have more time to be doing what I love to do. A lot of people started coming to me who had already been with this professional, or had attended this workshop, or seen this doctor who couldn't help them. So a lot of people came to me who had already visited the best people and they began to tell me what they needed. My whole work was based on NLP, but I combined it with their own intuition, focusing on asking the question of 'what is your own body intelligence telling you? What do you know is true or right for you?' When you listen, you can heal yourself. I am doing my PhD on this topic. That way, we could still stay on a scientific level and then I began to create my resilience methods.

During one month, a lot of women came to see me who were abused, so I found out what they needed so that they could heal their abuse and heal what they still had in their system – not only in the body, but also in their energetic system and in their mind on the basis of neuroscience. Then, another month, many people with Asperger's came and I thought, "Okay, then I need to find resilience tools for Asperger's." Then there was a soldier, who I had the pleasure to work with, and a lot of people who had traumas who couldn't find a way to deal with their challenges and I developed methods for them.

When I worked with other NLP master practitioners, really good ones, they asked me, "What are you doing and how are you doing it?" So they began to model some of my methods and copy me. When I am doing something intuitive, I am doing it from the unknowing part in me; with my subconscious. So they began to ask me, "How can we do what you do in the way you are doing it?" They began to model me. It was something that required my subconscious to become conscious, so I created many tools that other practitioners can use. At the moment, I am working with cancer patients. I have created resilience tools specifically for them. These are so simple that you only have to hear it once and you can do it right away.

Ironically, the biggest challenge that people have is not to learn my tools. The biggest challenge is to begin to listen to themselves again, rather than listening to others. They shouldn't listen to therapists, doctors, gurus, or anyone else, but be inspired by them to find their own way of living – they need to begin to listen to themselves. I would like the tools that I use in my intuitive coaching to become a well-known therapy in Austria and also abroad.

When I am working with clients, I am not judgmental. If a person believes in angels, I don't judge it. We take that and work with it. If a cancer person believes that an angel helps him or her to heal, and also wants to combine it with medicine therapy, then I will do that. I give them the space to allow them to be who they want to be. They are allowed to believe in whatever they want to believe. What I found when I worked with doctors is that they all have their norms and their beliefs and they insist on putting these beliefs into the minds of their patients. I don't do that and that's the huge difference between us and I think that's the reason why people are coming to me.

This topic is the main research field of my PhD studies: how the communication of people working in the health field is affecting their patients' health.

I've had this ability since I was a child listening to people in the bakery. I grew up with very old people around me because that was the clientele in our cafe. They told me stories about the Second World War and how it was back then. This was really very profound for me, so I listened to everything that was said. That was how my skills developed.

It doesn't matter what challenges my clients have. My deepest belief is that we will find a solution and that they will feel better afterwards. I'm using a larger part of the human consciousness because, as Sigmund Freud said, we only use 5% to 10% of our consciousness. Well, I use the rest of it. I have created tons of charts and materials to teach intuitive coaching tools to help people. I have some tools that are really profound; I call them emergency tools.

I did my further education in applied science in the field of health management and health promotion. That's why I called my tools 'resilience methods'. I needed a name that made it clear what I'm doing.

The nicest thing when I work with people is when their eyes begin to glow because they find themselves again. They have tools in their hands that empower them to help themselves. That's something very profound. It's beautiful when their eyes are glowing because they are happy inside.

So many people forget to have fun in their life. I saw it with the terminal care patients. They forgot to live their dreams because of their daily struggles for survival. Most people are just in survival mode and that's not fun. That's why I'm still doing what I'm doing.

All the people I've worked with have come through word-of-mouth recommendations because they were totally excited about the sessions. Then other people started coming to me. I never had to do any marketing.

Now I've started thinking about marketing outside of Austria so that I can have a global impact. I'm a senior programme and tool methods designer, so designing health tools and business tools and resilience tools comes naturally to me.

One of my biggest challenges is that I am a bit of an introvert, so it is a huge step to go global. But I feel I need to do this because I see how I make people happy with the tools I've created over the past 20 years and I know that it really helps other people.

What have been your biggest aha moments?

I learned to trust my inner truth and intuition even when there was a hurricane around me. I discovered that I could handle it when I stayed true to myself within my zone.

I started listening to my higher intuition – believing in something greater out there that is guiding me and taking care of me.

In the past, there was a time when I truly felt like I wanted to kill myself. It was an ugly feeling: the feeling when you really want to give up and believe that killing yourself is the only choice. But I realised that this was just not true. From this, I created very simple tools to help other people who might feel the same way. I think 99% is overthinking, rather than true feelings. You always have the choice to change your life.

What's been your biggest success or achievement?

For me, it's still being alive after the accident and all that happened.

Also, I was faced with a situation where I was pressured and belittled at work. I can't go into this in much detail for legal reasons. But I felt like I was pushed into leaving a company. It was a total shock. I almost gave up. I threw a lot of stuff away that I had created over 20 years because my entire belief in the goodness of the world broke down. I was thinking, "What can I change so that I can get back my belief that the world is still a nice place?" I began to think about what I really need in my life and what's really important and what's not.

After this happened, I began to hide myself away and went back to being an introvert. I was sliding backwards. Then I asked, "How can I create my life the way I want it to be and be who I want to be?" This inspired me to create tools for women so that they don't have to experience the same thing. For me, in every single obstacle and setback, there's always, always something good in it.

Tell me about your scientific research

My PhD is based on the fact that I always wanted my tools and methods to be scientifically proven. The basis of my PhD work is studies in communication and language science, with a focus on psycho-neurolinguistics and neuroplasticity. In layman's terms, this means everything that happens to me is based on my beliefs; on what I think is true or not. If I change my beliefs, my whole life will change. If I learn what I need to learn out of the obstacles, out of the hurricane moments, then I get a very different view and I can change it afterwards.

What advice would you give to other women wanting to achieve what you've achieved?

Stay true to yourself and listen to your female intuition, even when everyone is trying to break you down. For example, I could have carried on at the top management level, be living in a house in France, have my own horses and international clients. Instead, I checked what was actually important in my life. (Whatever is important in life is whatever *you* define. For me, it was my family and being grounded.) I really listened to myself.

By going on a sabbatical, I was able to prepare for something bigger to grow inside me. I was able to create my own nutrition work, my own intuitive coaching style and resilience. I go out into mother nature, meditate (next to my scientific PhD work), and do sport (functional training).

I keep giving myself time out and go with what I feel is right and perfect for me, even when I get 'wow' offers from others. I believe in being the 'inconceivable me' regardless of what everyone else thinks. You should never go below your own standards of what you believe is right for you. Even when your whole surroundings tell you something else and others choose those (lower) standards as their truth, be a wild woman going your way rather than being a sheep!

At the moment, I work with a lot of women in top management roles, but who are using coping methods more suited to men. Men are taught to be tough on the outside. I understand that and have that side of me also. It's important. But more important for women is to go a little bit deeper, to listen to ourselves, and use the female intuition that is our birthright.

When I work with women, what I find out most is that we don't give ourselves the space we need to actually hear ourselves again. Try to remember what you loved to do as a child to really live out your dreams. You are not only a mother or a worker. Just listen to yourself and what you love to do. Sometimes, when you have a hurricane around you, this is an opportunity to let go and begin to feel yourself again.

It doesn't matter what everyone else is saying. Instead, really begin to listen to yourself. Of course you will have a lot of obstacles. A lot of people won't like that you have begun to just be simply you. Free yourself. When we really use our female intuition, we can change the world.

My motto I choose for my work is simply: 'Nurture a woman and mother, and you nurture the whole world!'

LOUISE K. SHAW

"The body holds such a plethora of wisdom, if only we could stop the distractions that modern-day living have cultivated and set aside the time to tap into it."

Job Title: The Body Whisperer®

Personal Bio: Louise is an experienced energy psychologist and intuitive coach specialising in recovery strategies for consciously-motivated professionals feeling floored (or flawed) by the impact of the 3 D's: Death, Divorce, or a Diagnosis, transitioning them from turmoil to tranquillity. She uniquely achieves this by reconnecting them to the wisdom and healing powers within the body. It's also her passion to educate people about the bio-logical cause of depression, to inspire those who suffer from the symptoms to regain control of their lives and, ultimately, to empower them to create a magical future for themselves.

Services: Where you are in your journey will determine what you'll need right now. You may need support to manage the impact of the initial shock of a life event. It could be that you need help to get back on your feet to start addressing practicalities or emotionally adjusting to your new life. Or you may be ready to start making proactive plans for your future. No matter where you find yourself, Louise offers a solution for your individual circumstances. Her Awaken Your Mojo® Series includes a Group Coaching Programme and an Online Coaching Programme and she works with private clients on an individual basis.

Contact:

E: lks@louisekshaw.com

Website: louisekshaw.com

♦ ♦ ♦

My mum looked eagerly out of the window of the plane, searching for an airport. Beneath her, quickly coming clearer into view, was a wood and metal shack. As she nervously looked around, the realisation hit home that this shack was the airport. The arrivals, departures, and immigration building all combined under this small roof, presenting her first impression of the life she was entering into, as the plane landed in Dampier, in the Northern Territory of Australia. I was a little over 18 months old as she stepped off the plane to greet my dad, who'd arrived a few weeks earlier to get settled in.

Having parents who had chosen a way of life that was different to their peers was certainly a great foundation for my three older brothers and me. My dad was a role model for working hard to achieve what you wanted in life. His 6' 1" stocky build encased a man who was incredibly intelligent and he hid a wicked sense of humour behind his stern, reserved, and shy persona. In direct contrast, my mum was the happy-go-lucky, engaging, sociable influence on our lives. What she lacked in her physical stature, being only 5' 2," she made up for in her personality. Combined, the overriding message I remember receiving from them was that through hard work and determination, we could achieve anything we wanted in life.

Our exploration of the Antipodes didn't last long and when I was just over five years of age, the family returned to England. Moving home so often when I was younger positively impacted me in that I feel comfortable in new surroundings and enjoy meeting new people. It also gave me the 'wanderlust bug', which has fuelled my desire to explore and try new things out, in all aspects of my life.

Through the majority of my time in school, I believed there was something wrong with me – that I must be a horrible person – because from the age of 8, I became the victim of bullies. Transferring to high school at 11 didn't change anything: only the bullies changed. Although I didn't realise it at the time, I created a daily ritual of self-preservation, guarding what I said and being vigilant about how I acted and responded. The constant scoping of the environment to make sure I wasn't in danger meant that my fight/flight activators were permanently on and this led to a stressed-out nervous system and emotional overwhelm. It's very difficult for people who haven't experienced this to appreciate the impact it has on you. And whilst well-meaning friends and family gave the advice of not letting it bother me, and to ignore the taunts, it's not as simple as that. You become consumed by trying to work out why this is happening to you, what's wrong with you, and the constant questioning of 'what did I do?'

Unfortunately, my dad and I didn't have a great relationship when I was growing up, not helped by the fact that he spent so much time away from home, either in England, Saudi Arabia, or Egypt. I admired him from a distance and always wanted him to be proud of me, like any daughter would. One of his best friends was a barrister and I was really drawn to this profession. I remember avidly watching any programmes on TV that involved court cases and pictured myself one day standing in a courtroom presenting my case and sharing the truth. I followed in my youngest brother's footsteps and headed to grammar school to take my 'A' Levels, determined to study law at a prestigious university. I knew I had to take subjects I enjoyed if I was going to achieve good grades. I elected to take maths, geography, and art, and an 'O' Level in law. I remember being told to visit the headmaster and he explained that it wouldn't be possible to take art and maths together. He believed that I couldn't be good at both a creative subject and a logical one, and yet I stood my ground.

With such advancements in our knowledge of how the brain works and the optimum learning style, it amazes me that the majority of the schooling system is still following a template created during the Industrial Revolution. It's my belief that many of the children who are struggling in school today are feeling constrained and stifled by the structure of the learning environment. It's still prevalent from an early age to encourage children to pay more attention to their logical left hemisphere, rather than to tap into and listen to their creative right hemisphere. Importance is given to logical answers and evidence for the basis of decisions, rather than gut instinct and a sense of knowing – which is ironic, considering some of the most successful entrepreneurs, like Sir Richard Branson, have stated they favour gut instinct over facts and figures.

From my early days of wanting to be a lawyer, I was hooked on the ability to piece bits of information together and find the answer that would solve the crime or deliver the truth. Lower-than-expected grades meant that my dream of becoming a barrister was thwarted and, even though I was disappointed, I knew I would land on my feet. With a huge curiosity streak, and never being content to do something 'just because it's always done like that', I trusted these traits would enable me to forge a rewarding career for myself. The discipline and determination instilled by my parents led me to be the first woman to be promoted from trainee to Training Manager in just over a year in the Birmingham Division of Acuma - American Express's Financial Planning Division for high net-worth clients. Everything in my life was perfect and I was in my element.

It only takes a few seconds for your life to change dramatically, tearing a huge chunk out of you and knocking you completely off your feet. On 19 September 1991, I woke up to a scream that was so primal and raw, I jumped out of bed in sheer panic. It was the early hours of the morning and I stumbled down the stairs, unable to coordinate my feet, my heart pounding in my chest. If you were with me in the hallway on this autumn morning, you'd witness my father's stocky frame reduce in size as his body bent over. My mum is grabbing onto him, her petite frame crumbling from the words that the two strangers have just delivered. And even though she is screaming into my dad's chest, the intensity of my mother's distress had no chance of being absorbed by his body.

I don't remember the days after that morning. In fact, I don't recall much of the whole year. I was on autopilot; grateful for having a job to go to and yet not wanting to face anyone. Torn between days of bottomless tears and days when I felt so numb I just wanted to be swallowed up by the earth. It had been a distressing year. My mum lost her father on 19 March; my dad lost his aunt on 19 October. They both lost their youngest son on 19 September. What surprises me today is that I was never offered, or even sought, any professional help to manage the impact of three family deaths in one year. It was not even talked about in our family and everyone just seemed to be getting on with life. No one really had the emotional capacity to be there for each other, as we were all reeling in our own grief. Looking back, it's obvious that self-blame, regret, anger, and an indescribable sadness slowly started eating away at each remaining family member. This would ultimately destroy the bond that existed between us all.

Distraction works wonders for the short term. Yet, it becomes its own problem when relied upon for long-term resolution. A year after my brother was killed by a drunk driver, I realised I was just existing and not living. I jumped at the chance to meet a friend in Australia and in the end, I spent a year travelling around the world. When I returned, I followed many of my friends to London and embarked on a new chapter in my life. Within weeks of arriving, I'd secured a fantastic job in an innovative and fast-expanding company. Giddy with the excitement of London and the potential it offered, I started to believe my life was finally back on track. I'd been staying with my friend Sarah whilst I got my bearings and after a few months I moved into my own place. I loved my life! I had a well-paid job, a great social life, an amazing place to live just around the corner from work, and I was living the dream in one of the greatest cities in the world.

On one particular February morning, I was enjoying my walk to work as the sun was starting to rise. I was looking forward to the weekend as a group of us were heading to Sarah's parents' house in Dorset for a celebration. As I happily started planning my day, the phone rang and it was my closest friend, Mark. His voice was strange and he was finding it difficult to talk, which wasn't like him. He explained that Sarah had decided to drive down to Dorset last night to prepare for the weekend. She went later than normal to miss the traffic and whilst driving through the country lanes a man decided to overtake on a corner and drove straight into her. Sarah was killed instantly and on her best friend's birthday, the cause for the celebration.

Another common coping strategy when people experience pain is avoidance. Obviously, we are not aware that we do this and normally it results in pushing down feelings. In an attempt to not feel, this normally leads to feeling numb, which is how I felt for years. And I discovered that, in an attempt not to feel pain, I actually lost the ability to feel pleasure. To further distract myself from what I was feeling inside, I threw myself even more into my career, securing a management position in an international financial services company. Alongside this, I built a property portfolio worth over £1 million, all before I reached 30. At last, I had something in common with my dad and I enjoyed our discussions around property investing and my investment plans for the future. I was enjoying financial success and couldn't imagine anything rocking this boat. That was, until I returned off holiday in 2001.

My partner had proposed on holiday and I was excited to get back to work to share my good news with my colleagues. My first day back ought to have been full of celebrations; instead, I was advised that my team were to be made redundant. This wasn't entirely a surprise; how it made me feel was. I'd loved working with this company and even won a global award for creating a graduate recruitment and development programme. From being a positive person who always believed that I was really good at what I did, I fell into the trap of believing that I obviously wasn't that good, otherwise I wouldn't have lost my job. How we process the emotional impact of our experiences in life is a significant influencer in forming who we become. Unless we are consciously aware at all times, distressing events can lead to a never-ending cycle of self-blame and criticism. This, in turn, eats away at your self-esteem and confidence and before long, the downward spiral starts spinning out of control.

What's so insidious about it is that it makes you believe that everything around you, and everyone else, are the perpetrators in the drama that is enfolding.

Initially, I was delighted to be free of the corporate structure and it enabled me to follow my passion in property. I founded a home-finding business and qualified as a mortgage broker. Plans were progressing for my forthcoming wedding and those tinted glasses were looking rosy once again. With the benefit of hindsight, the roses were quickly becoming overgrown with thorns.

We have two very important parts to our brain: the conscious and subconscious minds. The conscious mind is responsible for the actions that we take in the present. The subconscious mind recalls programmes of learning and habits. For example, it will be your subconscious mind that recalls the programme that enables you to walk and talk. It's a good thing because you wouldn't want to have to relearn this every day! It also controls all the actions that enable you to live, like breathing or making the heart beat. All these are great, but there's another side. It also remembers all events in your life and, more importantly, what you felt about them or believed about yourself as a result of them. With every major event that unfolded in my life, it was reinforcing an overwhelming insecurity around not being wanted and believing that I'd always be abandoned by people I love. Here's the crucial part: when your subconscious believes something, it will go full out to prove it to you. Essentially, what you believe becomes your reality. I wish I'd learned about this in school; then, maybe, I would have spotted what was happening earlier.

The year I was due to get married was a year of emotional turmoil, instead of excitement in anticipation of the big day. The closer it came to sending out the invites, the more my stomach knotted. I was so in love with my fiancé and yet something didn't feel right and it's taken many years to understand what happened that year. You see, as I had a subconscious belief that people I love would abandon me, then I believed my fiancé would too. As a result, I needed to protect myself from being hurt and to stay in control I had to be the one who ended the relationship. Your conscious mind will execute the plan created by the subconscious mind and it will all seem totally logical and justified at the time. Yet on reflection, you'll notice the pattern and the limiting beliefs. This explains self-sabotage: why we attract the same toxic people into our lives; why we never reach the next level in our career; why we never stick to diets; why we are always broke ... the list goes on. Quite simply, if your life isn't turning out how you expected it to be, the chances are there will be limiting beliefs running in the background and your subconscious mind is being a loyal servant and delivering what you believe.

Have you ever been in the situation where you feel that you are operating on autopilot? That each day merges into the other, with nothing distinguishing them? If you were with me when I left my office on a cold wet evening in October 2005, you'd be getting into my two-seater Mercedes. The short drive home takes us to Greenwich, London, where you'd walk into the hallway of my beautiful Victorian home. Walking into the kitchen, you'd see me open the fridge door and pour myself a large glass of wine, my routine since the day my fiancé left. I turn on the TV and watch a repeat of *Titanic*. Jack is hauntingly similar in looks and character to my late brother and before long I'm in floods of tears. As Rose lets go of Jack's hand and watches him disappear into the depths of the ocean, I too feel as though I am being dragged to the bottom of the sea. I had all the material trappings of success and yet I felt dead inside. Rose knew that if she didn't let go of Jack, she would also die. In that moment, I knew I had to let go of everything I loved, in a similar way to Rose, and what I did next surprised me.

Hangovers are brutal and when I woke up, my head was splitting in two. Then I remembered what I had done the night before and nervously headed downstairs to the study. There, on the computer screen, were the words that would change the direction of my life once again.

Two months later, you'll find me sipping champagne on the Virgin Atlantic flight to Los Angeles. You see, that night I was drunk, I went to the computer and decided I would do whatever I typed. And those words were: Acting In L.A. Originally I planned to be away for six months, yet it turned into six years. I loved America, the sunshine, the positive attitude, the land of opportunity. I felt free and the happiest I'd been for years. Events led me to the Kabbalah Centre and the first day I walked in the front doors, I felt like I'd arrived home. The teachings of Kabbalah opened me up to a completely different world in terms of understanding the Universe, the Divine, our intuition, and the term 'consciousness'. It was the mysticism of Kabbalah that drew me and I craved the love given by the community. I sought out other teachers like Louise H. Hay, Dr. Wayne Dyer, Deepak Chopra, and Eckhart Tolle. I followed Joel Osteen every week on TV and travelled to see James Van Praagh and Marianne Williamson live. I had regular sessions with an incredible medium who explained with scary accuracy events that had happened in my life. I became fascinated with Esther and Jerry Hicks and Abraham completely challenged the concepts that I had grown up with. My mind was expanding and I was hooked to discover more.

In my second year of living in Los Angeles, I woke up one morning and literally fell out of bed in extreme pain from the middle of my back all the way down to my toes on my right side. I was scared because I'd gone to bed alright and I hadn't done anything over the previous few days that could have contributed to the pain. An MRI scan revealed an 8-mm herniated disc, which was pushing into my sciatic nerve, and the specialist explained that the only cure was to remove my disc. Not wishing to have surgery, for two years I saw a number of chiropractors. Whilst they relieved the pain temporarily, nothing was permanent. As a last resort, I agreed to have an epidural to relieve the pain. Instead, I literally crawled out of the hospital in Beverly Hills, in more pain than when I had walked in. My mind was made up; I didn't trust the opinion of the specialists and I certainly wasn't going to have surgery.

It was at this time that I had been seeing a hypnotherapist, Lynda Malerstein, about my anxiety. At the start of one session I was in so much pain, I asked if there was anything she could do to relieve it. She asked, "Do you want to try this technique that I'm learning? It's called Emotional Freedom Technique and we can give it a go." In that session, the pain literally jumped to the left-hand side and I remember saying, "Oh my word, the pain's moved! This proves it wasn't structural!"

I rushed home and continued to tap (using EFT) every day. Five days later, I was walking upright, the painkillers were in the bin, and no scalpel had touched a hair on my body. In that moment, it really dawned on me how powerful our body was to heal itself. EFT was created by Gary Craig, who started his career as an engineer and later trained as a Certified Master Practitioner of NLP. He became fascinated with ancient civilisations' knowledge around healing and combined this with the emerging insights around how the mind worked. As emotions are simply energy in motion, Gary realised that by stimulating the body's meridians, in a similar way to acupuncture but without the needles, you'd be able to release blocks in the energy flow. Once the blocks are released, the other key element is to make a cognitive shift in your perception of the event (using NLP techniques). This is exactly what I'd experienced. This alternative approach to healing has become so popular, it's being offered to NHS patients in certain parts of England.

In America, I had first-hand experience of healing myself from a chronic pain that lasted over two years, which the specialist advised could only be cured with surgery. When I had to return to the UK in 2011, as I couldn't extend my visa any longer, I was absolutely devastated. It felt like another failed relationship, and it was the trigger for an experience far worse than what I'd experienced in America.

In the western world, we have fostered a culture of believing that everything 'out there' will make us happy: that if we need a solution to any problem, then it can be bought or we can find it in other people. Even Hollywood has played a part in this, with its favoured line in romantic stories: 'You complete me!' or some derivative of this sentiment. But the fact remains that no one can complete you or make you feel wanted, loved, respected, or significant, other than the person you look at in the mirror every day. If you don't feel you are enough as you are, then no one around you will either. Social media has forced a false culture upon us to believe that everyone else's lives are perfect. It must be true because haven't you seen all the happy faces on Facebook and Instagram? What these photos don't show are the ruminating thoughts that are whirring around inside many people's minds, reminding them that they're 'not enough', in whatever way that translates to them.

The inner critic is the greatest cause of low self-esteem and it can be relentless in its barrage of insults every day. I know, because mine would have won the award for the most vicious attacks, in every waking moment.

Even though I'd achieved a Degree with a Major in Psychology, in America, so I knew how the mind worked, I couldn't seem to stop the deluge of negative thoughts, nor change my destructive behaviours. My life was spiralling out of control fast. I displayed all the classic symptoms of depression: insomnia, mood swings, irritability, addictions, anger bursts, overwhelm, loneliness, feeling helpless, anxiety, and withdrawal. My memory was all over the place and carrying out a simple task of returning a text felt like you'd asked me to climb Mount Kilimanjaro. I had become paranoid and was afraid to venture out of the house. My erratic behaviour was ostracising friends and, as a consequence, the cycle of self-criticism and blame became worse.

I finally acknowledged to myself that I was in trouble and if I didn't do something soon, I feared I would be living out the rest of my life in a mental institution or I'd take my own life. It was only at this breaking point that I remembered all about EFT and how it had helped me in the U.S.

I knew I wanted to be trained in the technique and came across Karl Dawson, who is one of only 11 EFT Founding Masters trained by Gary Craig. Just a month later, you'd find me sitting at the front of the hotel room in Brighton, waiting for Karl to start his training. This was the start of my journey into the fascinating world of Energy Psychology and Quantum Healing. The more I learned about how the body responds under stress and as a result of trauma, the more in awe I was of the vehicle I get to walk around in every day.

I recognise, now, that these days were the start of me fulfilling the most important job of my life, and that was to get to know who I was. For years, like many people, I had been playing a role that I had fallen into. I was always so busy with what was going on 'out there', there wasn't time to stop to look at what was going through my mind, let alone what was happening in my body.

I followed the conveyor belt of expectation: go through school, get further qualifications, find a job, get married, have kids, and live happily ever after. Except that, in following this path and trying to be someone else, I was suppressing every part of who I truly was. The masculine mask I'd adopted to compete in the male-dominated financial services industry had become so engrained, I believed it was the real me.

As I became more qualified in various modalities, it became frighteningly obvious how every loss I hadn't come to terms with in my life had impacted how I perceived myself and the world. Up until this point, I wasn't even aware of the grief cycle, let alone techniques to navigate its relentless rollercoaster of emotions. Early childhood abuse and years of bullying at influential times in my personality's development created a persona that quite simply just tried to survive. I'd become cautious of the words I used, of expressing my opinion, and even became neurotic about whether I was liked. I was desperate to be accepted and turned into a people pleaser at the expense of my own values. I sought constant approval for every decision I made, for fear of making the wrong one and it failing, or being criticised for my choices. When we lose our sense of who we are, through any major life event such as a death, divorce, or a life-altering diagnosis, these are the moments when it's essential to have the tools to be able to emotionally handle the impact of the trauma we experience.

We also experience trauma when our environment or territory is impacted and the territory can be our home or even our body. Your body is a sacred space and if anything violates this, whether under forced situations or not, how you interpret this on a subconscious level will determine whether the impact will stay in your body. It's obvious now that the events I experienced growing up were creating scars in my personality and with each traumatic event that I was unable to process, the scars grew larger.

In June 2005, Steve Jobs addressed Stanford University's graduating students and his commencement speech had a profound impact on me. He said, "You can't connect the dots looking forward; you can only connect them looking backwards. So, you have to trust that the dots will somehow connect in your future." My dots started to connect when I first became aware of Energy Psychology and trained to become a practitioner in Matrix Reimprinting and a trainer in EFT. These therapies enable you to join the dots of past events and understand how they influence your present day. I intellectually knew that the bullying had impacted my confidence, my health, and my outlook on life. Yet until I started using these techniques, I hadn't realised quite how much.

In the 1800s, Einstein stated that "Everything is energy and that's all there is to it. Match the frequency of the reality you want and you cannot help but get that reality. It can be no other way. This is not philosophy. This is physics." I've always known intellectually how important it is to be positive and yet I didn't understand about energy, vibration, and frequency. Therefore, I still hadn't grasped that my reality was only responding to my predominant thoughts. What intrigues me is that the ancient civilisations in the East knew about this thousands of years ago and yet it's only just being welcomed by certain factions of Western medicine. When I started to revisit memories from when I was bullied, I started to see a pattern in my energy. It was very defensive and aggressive and so I was attracting that behaviour from others. When I learned to release all the fear, anger, and hatred, and change it to the vibration of compassion and love, I was able to forgive the perpetrators and, more importantly, myself. This instantly changed the way I perceived the event and, quite often, the event in my mind changed as a consequence. Wouldn't this be a great technique to teach children, so that they could manage the way they feel about events that happen to them in that moment? If teachers and parents were equipped with these, too, then what an amazing experience it would be to support a child in releasing negative emotions and helping them change their perception of events.

It's funny how life turns out. All those years ago when I wanted to be a barrister to share my truth – it's actually coming true in a different way. My truth has come from personal experience and offers the perspective that your body is an intelligent organism. The body holds such a plethora of wisdom, if only we could stop the distractions that modern-day living have cultivated and set aside the time to tap into it.

My message isn't an easy one to share as people are still indoctrinated to believe that there is no connection between their thoughts and what's happening in their life, let alone in their body. The Newtonian perspective that regards the body as a mechanical entity that eventually wears out or gets broken is still being taught in medical schools. And yet scientists and many experts in the personal evolution field have established that our symptoms are an indication that our being (the body/mind/spirit) is out of balance. But this isn't something new because Hippocrates (who's considered the father of modern medicine) stated long before the birth of Christ that "Natural forces within us are the true healer of disease." In fact, there have been phenomenal examples of people curing themselves from life-threatening diseases and people walking even after a diagnosis of paralysis. They could only have achieved this as a result of an absolute belief in their body's ability to heal itself.

When Bruce Lipton, Ph.D., a cellular biologist, walked out of his tenure at Stanford University in America, he did so because his research was disproving everything that he was teaching his students. So significant was his research that he claims 99% of all disease is caused by our environment and, more importantly, our perception of our environment. Essentially, he discovered that it was our thoughts that created disease and not our genes, as he had originally taught. Dr Reike Gehard Hamer conducted extensive research into the real connection between our thoughts and symptoms long before Louise H. Hay published her internationally acclaimed book *You Can Heal Yourself.* Gregg Braden, an eminent American scientist, became fascinated by the ancient civilisations' healing techniques and started to integrate this wisdom into his own scientific research. Dr Robert Scaer and Dr Peter Levine conducted significant research into the connection between trauma, our perception of events, and symptoms in the body. The list goes on, and yet certain parts of the medical industry are still trying to discredit alternative approaches to health and healing.

The more I work with clients, the more I become fascinated by the body's intelligence and how it's not creating anything without a bio-logical reason. When you truly embody this, you can no longer be a victim of your circumstance and this places you firmly back in control of your health and your life. Your body is communicating with you all the time: with the way you are feeling, how you are standing – even the words you use indicate a deeper understanding of what's really going on. Essentially, there is little credence given to symptoms being a signpost to a deeper imbalance. Yet if we just returned to basics, to listen to our body to understand its language, we'd learn so much. Just like what happened a couple of years ago when I was in a session with a client. We were addressing anger that had been stored in her body and I had a flash of inspiration for us to have a conversation with some of her organs. As a result, she had a profound realisation about events in her past and her symptoms started to get better. It's because of the technique I developed as a result of this session that I am now known as 'The Body Whisperer'. The body intrigues me and every session opens up a whole new understanding of the secrets the body holds onto throughout our lives.

We are living in a fascinating era, with social media making the world a smaller place. We are experiencing a powerful influx of information and are often overwhelmed by the constant stream available to us. Paradoxically, I believe we're also living through one of the worst times in history. Steve Jobs created a platform with the iPhone which promised us a more connected world. He delivered, but at what cost? With our insatiable need to feel connected with the outside world, we have created what I believe is the plague of the 21st century. Walk down any street and you're likely to be bumped into by a person whose main focus is the metal and plastic they hold in their hands. Families convene in the lounge at night, not to talk about their days, but to sit oblivious to each other as their gaze is on one screen or another. Dating couples and friends have dinner together and yet the first ping that comes from their phone is enough to distract them from the conversation. I believe that disconnection is the plague of the 21st century. Disconnection from our friends and family, from our relationship with nature, and, even more disturbing, disconnection from our body and our true self.

We have been conditioned to believe that happiness can only be achieved by purchasing any number of things external to us. We have handed over control of our body to an industry that monitors its profits more than the harmful side-effects of its products. And we are told that many life-threatening diseases are not curable and their cause is still baffling even the greatest scientific minds worldwide. However, the solutions are staring us in the face.

My vision is to enhance the quality of people's lives by reconnecting them to their body's wisdom. Raising awareness about the real cause of depression and how to use your body's intelligence to heal from within is a big challenge. My biggest regret is that I didn't finish my online programme, called 'Awaken Your Mojo', before my dad passed away in February 2017. My dad had been suffering the symptoms of depression since my brother was killed, and this was compounded by numerous vicious verbal and physical attacks over the years by those he trusted. Even though his self-confidence continued to be battered down by life, he was a proud man who rarely asked for help. After several attempts to support him, I decided that if I asked him to check over the programme, then he would by default learn everything I'd discovered on my journey to heal. My dad knew the importance of being positive and yet he didn't connect the impact of trauma on his body. You have to understand that making a decision to be positive is processed by the conscious mind and provides short-term results. Resolving trauma can only be done with long-lasting effectiveness, by accessing the subconscious mind. Had he gone through the programme, he'd have realised that the only way his body was going to get back into balance and heal was by addressing the anger, sadness, resentment, guilt, shame that he was feeling as a result of the trauma of my brother's death, the betrayal he felt from those close to him, and profound sadness about how his life had ultimately turned out.

When I stood on stage in front of 1,500 entrepreneurs and business owners in Orlando in November 2016, I was sharing from personal experience how Hippocrates was right. That natural forces within us are indeed the true healers of dis-ease. I believe I was given the opportunity to experience both physical and emotional pain to such a degree, and that I was introduced to the concepts of energy healing, so that I can be the change that I want to see in the world. It's my perception that the human race is at a crossroads in respect of its evolution. We either continue to follow the path that we have been following for decades, the one marred with disconnection, dis-ease, and discontent, or we are bold and strong enough to change our direction and reconnect with what's important in life.

LAURA SPOELSTRA

"Being an egg donor was for me a way to help another woman, but it has given me back more than I could ever have imagined in my wildest dreams."

Job title: Chief Whatever It Takes To Get Things Done

Personal bio: Mother of girl/boy twins. A driven Dutchy who has worked and lived in the UK for over 25 years. My 'Getting Things Done' attitude, combined with a passion for people, has served me over various industries, from hospitality to barcodes, from infertility to legal services. My out-of-the-box thinking is fuelled by a belief that pretty much everything is possible if you put enough energy behind it.

Business: I currently have two hats: Founder of Egg Donor Matters and COO at Adam Carlton

Services: Independent adviser to fertility sector. Estate planning specialists.

Contact:

@Laura_Spoelstra

Website: www.lauraspoelstra.co.uk

♦ ♦ ♦

I was a very confident child. As long as I can remember – since my twin brothers were born and there were four children under the age of five – I have always had a very strong belief in myself. It was that self-belief that has carried me all through my life. That comes from what I thought was my normal upbringing but, as I grew up, I realised it was anything but normal.

Both of my parents were born in Indonesia, my brothers were born in England, my sister and I were born in Holland; my mother was and is an artist, and my father was a naval officer who ended up being the Rear Admiral. So, my family was very different to that of most of my friends and certainly my British friends. We had a Bohemian lifestyle in a military setting. Since I was very little, I wanted to become a brain surgeon; not because I'm in any way inclined to the medical field, but because it sounded like the most complicated thing to do. I always was attracted to complicated things. But my parents never said to me, “Well, why not a nurse?” or, “Why don't you try something easier?” Whenever I said I wanted to become a brain surgeon, they said, “Yeah, sure. Whatever.” That was it. They didn’t ask, “Have you thought of the 12 years required to study?” No, nothing like that. So, as far as I recall, if I wanted to become a brain surgeon I believed I could become a brain surgeon. Though later on, I realised that studying medicine wasn't for me, that attitude was pretty much what I grew up with. That was my normal and I never had any inclination to fit in or be restricted. My family never wanted to fit in – never tried. It was a bit of an ‘everything goes’ upbringing. This pretty much sums up my attitude through my entire life.

I did the normal school stuff. I was head of my class from the age of five. Head of my year. Head of the school committee. Team captain. That type of girl. Not in a pushy way; it was just the way it was and I thought that was quite normal. I loved school. I loved learning. I’ve great memories of my school years and my school friends. I still am in contact with some of them. So, I did well at school. I’m sure that made a difference and helped me enjoy school. After, I wanted to study law, but I quickly realised, “No, this is not for me." Again, when I said, "No, this is not for me. I don't want to finish university," my parents didn't say, "Are you insane?" They just took it quite easily: "Yeah well, whatever you set your mind to, you're going to achieve."

I always worked, even when I was at school and even when I was a student. But my first proper job was as an events manager at an international school football tournament that hosted 6,000 kids over a week in Amsterdam, sleeping in various schools, playing on different football grounds. My job was organising the logistics around that. The fact that I was the oldest of four made a big difference while organising. Organising runs in my veins. At that time, it made the national newspapers because it was quite unusual for a young woman to organise a football tournament. Even then, I thought, "What's the issue? I don't have to play it myself; I just have to organise it." That was my first job and I took some fantastic lessons out of it. One of those lessons is actually one of my aha moments – one of my defining moments.

When I worked in that company, I was the youngest woman and the only one who wasn't a secretary. I quickly realised the difference between male and female communication styles and behaviour patterns. I knew I was right on certain things, but I just couldn't work out why I couldn't get my message across. So, one week, I decided to sit back in all the daily update meetings and observe what the men were doing. I thought, "Right. That's it. I'm going to copy that style. I'm not going to use many gap words or say things like, 'Well, I believe that...' – the things that women tend to do." So, I started speaking in the language that men use. Men use numbers and tend not to use words or phrases such as 'I believe', or 'I think', or 'it is my opinion'. They're much firmer in their language. So, very early in my professional life, I adopted a more masculine way of communication, without losing sight of the fact that I'm a very female woman. I think that made a big difference for me.

I realised that if a person, or a woman, says, "Well, I think" or "I believe this", men switch off. Men don't care what you believe; they want to know the facts. It's not even that important if the facts are necessarily true. The men I worked with brought up their points with such confidence and in such a way that I thought, "That's the way to do it." I also learned not to apologise. They don't say, "I'm sorry I'm late. I'm sorry I'm keeping you from your lunch, I'm sorry if you can't hear me over the outside noise." They don't do any of that nonsense. Even to this day, I still use these methods.

Another aha moment was when I realised that my true passion was supporting others. If I can lead an organisation which is all about supporting others, then I'm at my best. When I realised that it's not about me, but about others, that's when things really started to fly.

Tell me more about your career path and how you got to where you are today.

I moved first to Germany and then to England in 1992. I started working for a blue-chip company, as a secretary initially, because they didn't think my qualifications were valid. So, I thought, “Okay, I’ll do the secretary position and then I’ll work my way up.” It helped that I spoke three languages at the time. My boss put me forward for promotion, but the HR Director said the immortal words, “You're too pretty to be a manager.” And I thought, “Oh, screw that. I'm never going to win that battle.” If you say I’m under-qualified or not smart or not determined, I can work with that. But if you use my good cheekbones as a limitation to my career, then I’m screwed because it’s just the way I am. I’m 5'11 and I tend to wear heels, and yes, I’m blonde, and whatever other superficial qualities you would like to mention. Most people do remember me, but it doesn’t always help. So, I went and started working for another company as a sales director. I realised as a result of that comment that I needed to be in charge of my own destiny. I did not want to work for anyone who might use my looks against me, as I wasn't going to win something that arbitrary.

I met a technical guy there and we decided to set up a company in the barcode sector. That’s what I did in 1994, during my first two years in the UK. He ran the technical side of the business and I did everything else; it was a good team. I did that for a couple of years, made some good money, and learned lots of lessons as well. When I was 20, I made a bucket list of things I was going to do in my life. I included all sorts of things on this list, from ambitions to skills to learn: moving abroad, setting up a company, writing a book, learning another language, and running a marathon. On top of that, it said: become a mum. I realised when I was 20 that I would have done everything – illegal, immoral, unethical, you name it – in order to have children. As it happens, I didn't have to do any of that. That's just how I felt.

In 1998, I had my twins and shortly after saw an item on television about egg donation. I thought, "I was prepared to do anything to have my children. Let's give something back." So, I decided to become an egg donor. At that time, it was most unusual. Later on, I did my egg donation, which to this day is one of the most wonderful things I've done. I wanted to help, but I couldn't even find information online. I had to go out of my way to find a support organisation. In fact, I had to track down the GMTV television producer, and say, "Remember two years ago there was a programme about egg donation? A bit of a long shot, but do you recall what that woman was called?" Anyway, they remembered and passed me on to the woman who turned out to be the chair of the support organisation – and, lo and behold, I became a trustee of that charity within some months. In 2004, some law changes were announced and all the trustees left because they thought donation would collapse in the UK as a result. With my sales and marketing background, I thought, "No, you're just doing it wrong. I'm sure we can change this." Basically, I ended up being the chair because there was only one other person; we were the only two left standing.

So, by now a single mother, I was raising three-year-old twins at the time, running a company, and becoming the chair of a national charity. My passion had always been within the IVF field and for egg donation and sperm donation. So, over a period of eight or nine years, I did both things: I made my money in the IT company but was the chair of this now-growing charity. There came a point when I said to the Trustees, "Guys, I can do so much more, but I can't do it in my capacity as the chair. I'm already working 20 hours on top of everything else. We need to work out if we can get funding from the Department of Health so I can develop this further." And that's what happened. I left the IT company; I sold my stake, which gave me some breathing space, and I became the Chief Executive of the National Gamete Donation Trust, which is the national body for egg and sperm donation.

My volunteer role became a full-time role. During that time, the team and I changed the charity. Under my leadership, we changed the face of egg donation and sperm donation in the UK. The UK was the only country in the world where donation didn't collapse following this law change in 2005. So, I was advising various stakeholders and other countries about what set the UK apart.

2016 and 2017 were Shakespearean years – death, divorce, depression, drama, deceit, you name it. So, I left and took a sabbatical early in 2016. That's it in a nutshell.

Explain a little more about the structure of the National Gamete Donation Trust you were chief executive of.

The National Gamete Donation Trust had effectively three organisations under it. One of them was raising awareness for egg and sperm donation, which was the core of the NGDT. Then it had the Donor Conceived Register, which is an organisation I took on that links donor-conceived people via DNA. We did that with King's College in London. The third leg was the National Sperm Bank. I set up the first national sperm bank three or four years ago, which was a fun but challenging project to do. It makes me think back to my childhood years when I said, "Mum, I want to become a brain surgeon." When I said I was going to set up a national sperm bank, people around me said, "Yeah, sure. Whatever you put your mind to, I'm sure it's going to happen." It was very complex, with many moving parts, but we did it and proved how it could work.

I am a disruptor. People don't like disruptors as it challenges and/or changes the status quo. Ultimately, that is what I am and always have been. Always against the grain, but in a very polite and nice way and mainly for a good cause – nevertheless, against the grain. One of the hard parts I've learned in general is that as much as people like to think they like change, if you really push them, most will go back into their default setting. Most people actually hate change; they're quite happy being what they are and where they are. As long as they get paid, they are actually very happy with the 9-to-5 mindset. I didn't realise that in the past. I thought, "Of course they want to make this work. Of course they want to solve this problem." I learned very quickly that quite a few people say one thing, but when they're pushed and challenged, they don't like it. It was fascinating and frustrating to observe. It was a challenging time. I had the 'honour' of being on the front page of The Daily Mail and page three of The Sun, in the same weekend, with a picture. My teenage children weren't too impressed. I made quite a few waves and it created a lot of spite. Not that it bothered me because I do realise that it says a lot more about these people. But, nevertheless, it hindered progress.

There was a headline of the Daily Mail, for instance, which read, 'NHS Funds Sperm Bank for Lesbians.' This was the Saturday headline; the first page was in the boldest letters you could possibly imagine. Apart from the fact that it wasn't the NHS and it wasn't for lesbians, it created the most amazing uproar and even Katie Hopkins jumped into the fray. My face or name was everywhere you don't want it to be. It was the people against NHS-funded fertility treatment that spoke out, asking why we should fund lesbians and who wanted babies from Birmingham anyway! Some people in my field never quite understood why an outsider – although I am known and respected – should be trusted with setting up the sperm bank. I'm fully aware many in and outside the sector were against it: not necessarily the bank but more the organisation or, more to the point, me. Criticism was often very personal and I realised I couldn't win against that kind of criticism. Not that it bothered me; it was more an awareness.

Would you say that was one of the hardest challenges you've had to deal with over the years?

Being in the media generates all sorts of emotions. Anger, spite, envy, and only sometimes admiration. I think that my confidence in handling the media was a double-edged sword. It was recognised that it was needed to raise awareness, but there was irritation because of it too. I think that's what annoyed some people – my attitude of, 'Throw it at me. I don't care.' I was happy to debate on television and radio.

Ultimately, the biggest challenge out of everything I have done is combining raising my children with my work. That has always been my biggest challenge. Workwise, I've always had to justify and defend myself – perhaps because I'm a foreigner and an outsider. When I was younger, it was because I didn't look like an authority figure. There was always something that made me stand out, so I always had that initial hurdle. I was always too this, too that. Too present, too outspoken, too not like the others. Then, eventually, I would start hearing, "Oh, she actually knows what she's talking about. She's actually nice. She's actually very determined and disciplined." But, at first, I'm sure there's something about me that makes people uneasy.

In many cases, I wasn't the obvious choice, but it's part of why I do what I do. It's part of why I've become who I've become. I dealt with those things, and it made me stronger. The more things you do like that, the bigger your harness becomes and the more you grow. I started saying, "Ah, I've done this before, and I can do it again."

For a long time, Jon Snow was my 'I can do this' yardstick. For a Channel 4 live news interview with Jon Snow, they had initially asked the Minister and she wasn't able to do it. So, the Department of Health rang me and said, "Listen, they're really annoyed off with us, they need someone, can you do it?" I said, "Yeah, sure." They gave me half an hour's notice: luckily, I had a good hair day. They were clearly pissed off that they had me instead of the Minister and it came through in his questions. I was just the spokesperson of a national charity at the time. So, for a long time my attitude was, 'I've done Jon Snow live, so I can do anything.' Nothing can come any worse than Jon Snow live on Channel 4 News trying to grill me. Everything is peanuts after that.

Tell me about your work today as an independent fertility advisor.

The funding for the charity I led for 15 plus years has pretty much ceased. I set up an organisation, Egg Donor Matters, because there is still a need for an independent body dealing with egg donation so I'm going to fill that gap. During my sabbatical, I had to think, "Do I want to go back into this field or am I going to do something else?" I could have done many other things, but I realised that egg donation is my passion. So, I stepped back into it, but I wished to retain my independence so that I can continue doing other things.

My other focus is on business development for an estate planning solicitor firm. It's a completely different sector, but in the end it's all the same really: dealing with people and making things work.

My passion is still with egg donor and fertility issues. Interestingly, I was at the annual conference of the legislator HFEA yesterday. The people I spoke to there said, "Thank God you're back; it's much needed." So, I have faith that this will all work and that the organisation will be able to fill a role, or a gap, that we have at the moment. There is no independent information for patients and that's even more needed in the global infertility sector, where people just travel abroad to get their egg donors without knowing what's going on.

Who are the people you are helping day to day?

I help anybody who wants to become a parent via egg and sperm donation, mainly egg donation. I am trying to help patients to make informed choices in their fertility journey. Many clinics have an agenda that patients do not know about and I understand issues that most patients won't know about.

To explain more: what happens is that it's very hard to find egg donors in the UK; it's not impossible, but it's hard. There are some very successful clinics that do this. However, quite a few clinics, who can't be bothered, say that there are no egg donors in the UK and they refer their patients to clinics abroad. What patients do not realise is that many of the clinics get a referral fee. So, if a clinic gets £1,000-1,500 per referred patient to a foreign clinic, then of course the clinic in the UK is not going to recruit themselves, because they would miss out on a stream of income. It's an unseen stream of income from the patient's point of view and in the fertility world it's one of the elephants in the room. Many people do know about it, but nobody says it out loud and that's exactly what I'm planning to do: I'm going to say it out loud. I'm going to challenge them to be transparent so patients can make better-informed choices. This matters for all the patients because donors in nearly every other country they refer to are anonymous.

Now that there's DNA testing, it's almost impossible to guarantee anonymity for a donor. Especially with egg donation, we know that many patients, although they intend to tell that child throughout the course of their life, actually do not find a comfortable narrative to tell their child. They simply do not know how or do not want to tell the child that he or she was donor-conceived. Therefore, many parents effectively live with a lie. They don't tell the child that one or two of the parents are not the genetic parent. These children are very likely to find out. But clinics don't flag this up. They say, "You should use a donor from Spain; it's anonymous; your child will never find out and you don't need to tell the child." Well, these clinics shouldn't say that, because that's not the case.

Through running the Donor Conceived Register, I've been dealing with donor-conceived adults who say, "You know, it's been one of the biggest gaps in my life that I do not know anything about my donor. I don't want him or her to be my replacement parent. I don't need birthday presents or cards, I just want to know..." Sometimes they want to say thanks to them and other times they just want to know where their curly hair comes from, or why he or she is the only one in his or her family that's got musical talent. To not give people the opportunity to know where they come from, their genetics, is a real source of communal pain. But patients who are trying to get pregnant are so focused on that and that's understandable. They live from month to month: they know the fee, they take the temperatures, and so on – but they do not think of what happens when the child is 16 and starts to pick up the fact that there is a genetic mismatch in his or her family. Parents do not realise how much heartache and pain that can cause for the child, but for themselves as well, when they realise that it was a lie.

Nowadays, through DNA testing, it's very likely that their child will find out. However, these patients are not being told these downsides as they flick through the books of donors saying, "Oh, let's pick number 123 because she sounds very attractive." Their sole focus is getting pregnant so they don't think about the disadvantages. It's not in the clinic's best interest to share these disadvantages because, in many clinics, they just want the patient to get pregnant and pay the fee. It's not an easy message to hear as a patient, but at the moment they don't even hear it all. I spoke to quite a few people yesterday who said, "It's about time somebody stands up and says it." But, at the moment, there's nobody who can do it because some of them in the legislature know about it, but they can't really name and shame. Clinics will not comment on what their commissions are and on the profit they're making. I don't know the full extent of their reasoning. But that's why I'm doing it.

You mentioned that you donated eggs yourself – have you ever met the people you donated to?

No, I've never met them and I don't know who they are. I donated when I was 34 and I know that there were 13 good eggs in my cycle. At this stage, I know that I've achieved many more donations as a result of my work. I'm not sure I'd want to know what happened as I would be absolutely gutted if I found out that it hadn't worked at all. I still like to think that it was successful. Statistically, it's not 100% certain, by the way. In short, I don't want to know.

You've had many achievements over the years. What do you feel has been your biggest success and what are you most proud of?

I would say staying sane in an insane world and not losing my marbles is a huge accomplishment. I am also quite proud of still being close with my now adult children despite the fact that I'm a working mum. Also, despite the hurdles, and despite my age and despite everything else, I'm just as hungry for making a change as I was when I was 20. I could say individual accomplishments such as the companies, or the National Sperm Bank, or the fact that I moved abroad, but in general it's more that if I look back, I think, "Well, I kept going and I actually did so by keeping friends and family close to me and without pissing too many people off."

What advice would you give to other women wanting to achieve what you have?

Every journey is different. What worked for me was trying to improve myself on a day-to-day basis and using myself as a yardstick. As long as I'm better now than I was last week, or as long as I've learned something new, every day is another step. The other thing that you should do is make sure you are surrounded by good people –people who support you. They may not always understand you, and it's true that fewer people understand you the higher you reach, but as long as they accept and support you, you'll be fine. I'm a people person and I've always worked with people. I've learned that I'm best at supporting others and helping others in whatever journey they have. But I can do that because I'm supported myself by others. I have learned that if you want to do something fast, go on your own. If you want to go far, go with others. That's not necessarily just in work, but in general.

When I was about six or seven, I was with the Brownies and we were all given a Brownie name. All the other girls had some fancy name – Lily, Rose Petal, or some other equally cute name. My parents, of course, chose the best name for me. It was Wanting To Know It All. So, I was known as Brownie-Wants-To-Know-It-All. At the time I thought, "Really?" because all the other girls had pretty names, but I realise now that was the best name that they could have given me. The one thing I do every day is learn. I love to read and learn new information. I think that's what you need to do to stay on top of your game and to keep developing yourself. That's the advice that I would give to any person at all who wants to have an extraordinary life. Just keep learning.

What helps you get out of bed every day in spite of the tough times?

I know I am very blessed. I'm blessed with a great family, great children, great health, great friends, innate confidence, a good mind, and a happy outlook on life. I always wanted to share my good fortune. That's always been my drive. I originally wanted to be an egg donor for one reason: I wanted another woman to experience the joys of motherhood. That drive to make people happy underpins a lot of what I do. It sounds a bit soppy, but basically that's what it is.

I'm with the Samaritans as well, and one of the reasons is because I realised I'm very blessed that I have plenty of people to talk to. I have good friends who really know the shitty bits and I can talk to them. Nowadays, I hear so many people who don't have that and I want to share my blessing. It's as simple as that.

Do you consider yourself to be extraordinary?

When I was young, there was one line in a poem that triggered my bucket list. It was a Dutch line: "Groots en meeslepend wil ik leven", which means "I want to live big and bold."

When I was in school, I already knew that I didn't want to live an ordinary life or be ordinary. My life's definitely not been ordinary, but I'm not sure if I'm extraordinary.

I'm not coy or shy about it; I'm proud of myself and I'm a kick-ass woman. But through my life, I've met so many people who are extraordinary: amazing women who are foster parents, others who do amazing things as volunteers, doctors who changes lives, women who are surrogates, I find those roles really extraordinary, so I wouldn't want to put myself in that category.

I know other people find me extraordinary. I just believe that I'm blessed.

You do a lot of public speaking, raising awareness about fertility issues. Tell me about this.

Well, I've spoken at the biggest conference in fertility, The European Society of Human Reproduction and Embryology, which is very unusual considering I'm not an academic or clinician. I was one of the outsiders there, but I've done it twice, in Stockholm and in Lisbon. I think my best gig was when I was flown to Vancouver for a 20-minute Q and A session. I've spoken at quite a few conferences here in the UK. I've also done a lot of speaking in the media: that's where much of my speaking experience comes from.

I've been very privileged. I was sharing notes with one of my friends who was invited to Downing Street, and one of the exciting things for me is that I was asked to advise one of the foreign delegations in the UK. They were speaking to blood transplant groups and other organisations; I was one of the speakers. I was in the Foreign Office, we had an hour spare and the liaison officer asked, "Do you want me to show you around?" So, we all said, "Yeah, sure." So, I was able to walk around and see the ambassador rooms – rooms with huge elephants made of marble, the works. I realised that I had seen the inside of offices that many British people would never see.

I have also been a witness for a Joint Committee in the House of Commons. Again, I was inside there and I had another I-need-to-pinch-myself moment. Because I am a foreigner who just happens to be very passionate about something, and because I like helping others, I am able to see the inside of where it all happens in Westminster and the

Foreign Office. I still remember that and think, "Wow, just because I want to help people, this happened. Look at how I'm blessed." Being an egg donor was, for me, a way to help another woman, but it has given me back more than I could ever have imagined in my wildest dreams. It changed my career, it changed my life, it changed my circle of friends, and it changed my experiences. This all happened because I decided to become an egg donor and I find that one of the most amazing things.

WWW.POWERHOUSEPUBLISHING.COM